THE RADICAL WORSHIP SOLUTION

Igniting The Heart of Your Team

Austin Ryan

Worship Catalyst Inc.

For information contact;
Worship Catalyst
PO Box 751904
Las Vegas, NV 89136

www.worshipcatalyst.com

Cover design by Gary Gnidovic
Layout by Ben Lunn

ISBN: 978-0-9967145-0-1
First Edition: September 2015

CONTENTS

Foreword

By Eric Michael Bryant

Heading off to college can be an exciting and scary time in someone's life. College is a chance to discover yourself, pursue your career, and become an adult. At the same time, college freshmen have to wrestle with freedom. As a result, they have a choice to make: they can finally do everything they've always been told to avoid or they can continue down the intended path that leads to success.

For those of us who follow Jesus, we have seen far too many college freshmen wander from their faith and into trouble. Sometimes, we've seen those same kids return to Christ once they mature a bit or get into enough trouble.

As a college freshman, I avoided the pitfalls of freedom in large part because I met a cool sophomore who decided to use his freedom to invest in new students. I met Austin Ryan.

From the first time I met him and all through my college years, I wanted to grow up to be like Austin. I wanted to have the same kind of vibrant and authentic relationship with God that I saw in him. I wanted to have the same sort of passion he showed for serving others through the church.

For the past twenty-plus years I have been able to share a friendship with Austin. Whether he was investing in college students, leading worship in a small or large church, raising up worship leaders and creatives through Worship Catalyst, or planting a church in Las Vegas, Austin has continued to inspire and challenge me to become a better version of myself so that others will experience the love of Jesus.

Now, through this book, we can all learn from Austin the *Radical Worship Solution*. This message is critical. In our post-Christian world, the future of the church depends on our willingness and ability to connect others personally with the Creator of the universe. Austin does an amazing job of helping us to create a worship experience that removes the distractions of our busy world and helps us encounter our transcendent and incarnate God.

Through this book, we can experience personal and corporate renewal by applying the seven values: excellence, creativity, unity, humility, authenticity, evangelism, and party.

Our world needs what Jesus has to offer through his church— and I'm grateful Austin Ryan is one person who is directing us to discover Jesus in new and empowering ways!

—Eric Michael Bryant, pastor at Gateway Church in Austin, Texas, holds a D.Min. in entrepreneurial leadership and is author of *Not Like Me: A Field Guide for Influencing a Diverse World*. www.ericbryant.org

CHAPTER 1
Band Practice

Unfortunately, the following scenario plays itself out in churches all across North America on a frequent basis. Is this how your band practice sometimes goes?

Tuesday night, 6:50 p.m., main worship room in church. Worship Leader Eddie is plugging in cables on the platform. The other band members have not yet arrived.

New band members Taylor and Robert enter. Robert carries a bass guitar. Eddie notices them and walks over to greet them.

WORSHIP LEADER EDDIE: Hey guys. Glad you made the team and are joining us this week! You're even early!

NEW GIRL TAYLOR: (*startled*) Yeah, I thought practice started at seven.

WORSHIP LEADER EDDIE: It does. Did you get the music I sent?

New Girl Taylor: Yeah.

New Guy Robert: Uh-huh.

Worship Leader Eddie: Okay, cool. Did you understand my notes about the transition from the bridge to the last chorus on the first song? We're going to start small and go big during the four bridge repeats. Normally we just do three, but we're going to try four this time.

New Guy Robert: Yeah, sure, that's no problem. Where do I plug in my bass and stuff?

Worship Leader Eddie: Over here. There's a plug right here. If you want to just tune up, we'll get started pretty soon. Sometimes we have a few late arrivals.

New Guy Robert: Oh really?

Worship Leader Eddie: Yeah. We never start on time.

Singer Shelly and Alto Amy arrive. Shelly moves quickly to the stage, opens her laptop, and begins to work. Amy sees Taylor.

Alto Amy: Hi, are you the new singer?

New Girl Taylor: Yeah, that's me.

ALTO AMY: Great. Welcome. You're not here to take my spot are you? (*laughs*)

NEW GIRL TAYLOR: No, no, of course not! You guys do such an amazing job every week. I'm just excited to be here with everybody. I love this church.

ALTO AMY: How long have you been coming?

NEW GIRL TAYLOR: About two months.

ALTO AMY: Wow, not long at all. I'm sure this will be a good experience for you—especially still being on your honeymoon and all.

NEW GIRL TAYLOR: What?

ALTO AMY: What?

NEW GIRL TAYLOR: You said something about my honeymoon. What do you mean?

ALTO AMY: Oh, nothing. It's just great to see the newbies like you in love with the church and the band and all

NEW GIRL TAYLOR: You're not?

ALTO AMY: Not what?

New Girl Taylor: In love with the band and church and all?

Alto Amy: Oh sure. I've been here since I was twelve. In fact, I was the last person to be baptized in the old horse trough before we built this building. It's a great place as long as you know your way around the people.

***

7:00 p.m. Worship Leader Eddie has gone off to find cables. Drummer Dave arrives, carrying his drumsticks and music. He sees New Guy Robert.

Drummer Dave: Hey. Name's Dave. Good to have you. Eddie told me there was a new bass player coming around soon.

New Guy Robert: Hi, I'm Robert.

Drummer Dave: Cool. Been playing long?

New Guy Robert: I've been in and out of bands since high school, but when my wife and I had a kid, that kind of ended my run. So I haven't really played much in the past seven years.

Drummer Dave: Like riding a bike, right?

New Guy Robert: I hope so. We'll see.

Worship Leader Eddie arrives back in the room carrying random cables.

WORSHIP LEADER EDDIE: Hey, everybody, you ready to get started? I just need to plug in these drum mics. (*Starts running cables as the team watches.*)

ALTO AMY: Parker isn't here yet . . . of course. He's the typical brooding lead guitar player. You'll see.

NEW GIRL TAYLOR: Typical?

ALTO AMY: Yeah, you know—stays to himself, doesn't really talk to anybody, seems mad all the time, and never on time for anything. One time he walked in ten minutes before the service started.

NEW GIRL TAYLOR: Wow. What time are we supposed to get here?

ALTO AMY: The problem is his girlfriend. She almost never comes to church. I think they stay up really late on Saturdays. Did you ever see the movie Beetlejuice?

NEW GIRL TAYLOR: You mean from the '80s? Yeah.

ALTO AMY: You know the goth girl—the daughter in the family who moves into the house?

NEW GIRL TAYLOR: I think I remember her.

ALTO AMY: (*searches on her phone*) I'm going to find her picture. Dave, Parker's girlfriend looks like this, right?

DRUMMER DAVE: He's got a girlfriend? Is that the girl from Beetlejuice? (*sings*) "Daylight come and me wan' go home."

WORSHIP LEADER EDDIE: Hey Dave, where do you plug in your kick drum pedal?

DRUMMER DAVE: Shouldn't we have a sound guy here tonight?

WORSHIP LEADER EDDIE: Yeah, it's actually supposed to be Maddie, but her final psych paper is due tomorrow, or something like that.

DRUMMER DAVE: Don't we have other sound people?

WORSHIP LEADER EDDIE: No, she's it right now.

DRUMMER DAVE: What about that guy who always wears cowboy boots?

WORSHIP LEADER EDDIE: You mean Walter? He moved like three months ago. It's just Maddie now.

DRUMMER DAVE: Isn't she a little old for school?

WORSHIP LEADER EDDIE: Well, she always wanted to get a degree, but life happened. She's finally going back to college.

DRUMMER DAVE: No wonder these mics aren't plugged in yet.

NEW GUY ROBERT: Do you need help? I've set up a few sound systems before. I used to run sound for this monthly concert in the park thing where I used to live.

WORSHIP LEADER EDDIE: That would be great. Can you head back to the soundboard and start tracking down these channels?

NEW GUY ROBERT: Sure.

Alto Amy starts texting and laughs each time she receives a text response. New Girl Taylor sits on the front steps of the platform and looks through the music for the night's practice.

WORSHIP LEADER EDDIE: Okay, Dave, play the kick. Robert, are you getting that?

NEW GUY ROBERT: No. What channel is it supposed to be?

WORSHIP LEADER EDDIE: I think like ten or eleven.

Drummer Dave starts playing the whole drum kit now.

NEW GUY ROBERT: (*yelling to be heard over the drums*) I DON'T SEE IT COMING THROUGH. HAVE YOU CHECKED TO SEE IF THE MIC CABLE IS OKAY?

WORSHIP LEADER EDDIE: IT SHOULD BE. I JUST USED THESE LAST SUNDAY!

New Guy Robert: WHAT?

Worship Leader Eddie: THEY SHOULD BE OKAY. DAVE, CAN YOU STOP FOR A MINUTE?

Drummer Dave: (*stops playing*) Geez. You don't have to yell. I'm right here.

New Guy Robert: I don't have anything coming through the system. Can you come back here to see if it's plugged in right?

Sound girl Maddie enters and stands behind Robert.

Sound Girl Maddie: The amps aren't on.

New Guy Robert: (*startled*) Oh, thanks. I'm Robert. I don't really know what I'm doing.

Worship Leader Eddie: You made it! So glad you're here.

Sound Girl Maddie: I figured I could get you started; I just can't stay long.

Worship Leader Eddie: No problem. We're trying to get the drum mics working.

Alto Amy: (*into microphone*) Test. Test. Test. Is this on? Can you guys hear me?

***

7:10 p.m. Taylor notices Shelly working at the front of the stage and approaches her.

New Girl Taylor: Hi. I'm Taylor.

Singer Shelly: Oh hey. I'm Shelly. Are you the new singer? I think Eddie sent an email about you.

New Girl Taylor: Yeah, that's me—just getting started.

Singer Shelly: Welcome to the team!

New Girl Taylor: I saw you sing the first week I was here but haven't seen you since.

Singer Shelly: When was that? Like two months ago?

New Girl Taylor: Yeah.

Singer Shelly: Yeah, that's about right. Eddie doesn't schedule me very often. I travel for work quite a bit so I'm not in town much.

New Girl Taylor: How long have you been on the team?

SINGER SHELLY: Almost since the church started. I'm a carryover from the old regime.

NEW GIRL TAYLOR: Regime?

SINGER SHELLY: You know, there was a worship leader here for a while who ended up getting in an argument with the pastor and he left and took most of the band with him.

NEW GIRL TAYLOR: I didn't know that. What was the fight about?

SINGER SHELLY: I tried to stay out of it. I think it had something to do with "creative" differences. Scott was his name. He liked to push the edge. Amy would probably know more. She keeps her ear to the ground more than I do for things like that. Plus, she sings every week.

NEW GIRL TAYLOR: I guess she doesn't travel like you do?

SINGER SHELLY: (*shrugs*) I'm not sure why she gets to sing as much as she does.

NEW GIRL TAYLOR: She's been here awhile too. I guess you guys have been through a lot together.

SINGER SHELLY: Yeah, we have . . . we've been singing here for a while.

NEW GIRL TAYLOR: Well, it's nice to meet you.

Singer Shelly: Yeah, you too.

New Girl Taylor: Think we'll start soon?

Singer Shelly: Never can tell. I have some emails to finish so it's working out for me.

***

7:15 p.m. Drummer Dave leaves the room. Worship Leader Eddie is now back on stage trying different cables in different channels, while Maddie and Robert keep trying to make the soundboard work.

Worship Leader Eddie: Hey, Dave, try the kick drum aga… (*notices Dave is gone and sighs irritably*). Where's Dave?

Guitar Kid Parker enters from direction Dave left.

Guitar Kid Parker: I just saw him in the bathroom.

Worship Leader Eddie: Oh, hey Parker. When did you get here?

Guitar Kid Parker: Just a couple minutes ago.

Alto Amy: (*sarcastically*) Glad you could make it, Parker.

WORSHIP LEADER EDDIE: (*genuinely*) Yeah, me too. Can you come over here and play the kick drum? I'm trying to get these things to work.

GUITAR KID PARKER: Sure.

WORSHIP LEADER EDDIE: (*shouts to Maddie*) ANYTHING?

SOUND GIRL MADDIE: Yeah, I got it. Finally.

WORSHIP LEADER EDDIE: (*signals for Parker to stop*) Thank goodness!

ALTO AMY: Now that we have that working, can you get this mic turned on, Maggie? Test, test, test. Helloooooooo. Helloooooo.

Drummer Dave reenters.

DRUMMER DAVE: Why didn't these mics stay plugged in from Sunday?

WORSHIP LEADER EDDIE: The church had a big outreach last night and had to clear the stage for it. We were giving out clothes and toys to some of the neighborhood kids, and there was a guy from the city council who spoke. It was really cool.

ALTO AMY: Couldn't they do that without clearing the stage?

WORSHIP LEADER EDDIE: We talked to Pastor John about that, but they really needed the space for this dance group that performed.

DRUMMER DAVE: Did they do "Thriller"?

WORSHIP LEADER EDDIE: Actually, they did do part of "Thriller"! It was mixed in with some other famous dances through the years. They did a pretty good job.

ALTO AMY: Here? That's surprising! I'll bet there were a few raised eyebrows.

WORSHIP LEADER EDDIE: Not many of our people were here. But it was packed with folks in need from the community. Pastor John got to talk at the end and several people raised their hands to start a relationship with Jesus.

Silence for a few seconds as people, obviously embarrassed for not being there, look at the floor, ceiling, etc.

NEW GIRL TAYLOR: That's great, Eddie! Maybe some of them will come back for church this week.

WORSHIP LEADER EDDIE: I hope so.

Eddie finishes up the cables and checks the rest of the drum channels.

***

7:30 p.m.

WORSHIP LEADER EDDIE: Okay, guys, I think this is finally done. Are you all ready for a sound check?

ALTO AMY: Ugh. Finally! Check, check. Is this on? Can you hear me? Maddie, I changed the batteries.

SOUND GIRL MADDIE: Okay, Amy. I got you. Shelly, could you talk into your mic?

SINGER SHELLY: Yeah, hang on. *(finishes an email, stands, takes her mic)* Hello. Test.

SOUND GIRL MADDIE: Good. Bass?

NEW GUY ROBERT: *(plays his bass)* I didn't really know where to plug in. Is this good?

SOUND GIRL MADDIE: Yep. Lead guitar?

GUITAR KID PARKER: *(plays his guitar very loud)*

SOUND GIRL MADDIE: HEY! PARKER, CAN YOU TURN THAT DOWN? A LOT?

WORSHIP LEADER EDDIE: CAN YOU HEAR THIS GUITAR? AND MY VOCALS?

SOUND GIRL MADDIE: YES! I— *(nods, refusing to yell anymore, gives a thumbs up, and then walks out of the building.)*

WORSHIP LEADER EDDIE: (*into microphone*) OKAY, GUYS, LET'S GET READY TO START!

The players find a natural place to stop the impromptu song and things quiet down.

WORSHIP LEADER EDDIE: Okay, so why don't we pray to get started?

CHAPTER 2
The Solution

Do you feel stressed after reading chapter 1? Are your muscles tighter than they were just a few minutes ago when you started going through that script? It would be great to say that this is a far-fetched, crazy, unrealistic story. But if you and I are honest, we could say that portions of this drama hit a little too close to home.

Maybe you have experienced busybodies on your teams like Alto Amy who love to know all the juicy information so she can let everybody know what she knows. She thrives on controversy and gets her energy from seeing people in crisis. Her food is control and she is not about to let anyone else consume it. Few people trust Amy and she continues to push them even further away.

You probably know Drummer Dave. He believes everything should be a certain way and everyone should work hard to make it right—until he has to lift a finger to fix something himself.

How about Singer Shelly? She is a hard worker who has little extra time. She does ministry on her own terms when she can fit it in, but she also feels left out. She puts on a tough outer shell, but inside she wants to be needed.

And then we have Worship Leader Eddie. Needless to say, he is in over his head with this cast of characters. He seems to be frighteningly close to the edge just trying to make sure the whole ministry doesn't explode. Eddie has a good heart, but it seems this band is leading him down an unhealthy path. My guess is that Eddie stays up some nights wondering how to get this team under control.

When leaders like Eddie experience these types of team dynamics, they often don't know where to start to improve things. It seems as if they have too many problems to solve and too many relationships to fix. A leader in Eddie's position might even think that this one night of practice is the problem. But one night is almost never the problem. This one night was a symptom of something much bigger.

A Unique Approach

For more than twenty-five years I have been the point worship ministry leader in churches small and large. After leading well over one hundred creative artists in a church in Texas, my wife, Cami, and I began to notice, that when new churches started, more than half of them had no worship leaders. We knew that what we experienced in our established church was great, but we also knew that we had to find a way to help these newer, gospel-centered churches. The cry of church-planting pastors became too strong. So in 2007 we founded an organization called Worship Catalyst.

Since then, our team, including ministry hubs in more than fifteen locations, has worked with churches throughout the United States and Canada. We walk beside church-planting pastors and help them build worship teams; training them and discipling the arts-ministry team leaders. Along the way we have spent many hundreds of hours dialoguing with worship leaders, pastors, creative artists, and business leaders about how to effectively build teams and connect their congregations to Jesus. In the vast majority of these conversations, the same challenging issues come up over and over again.

You and I and every other leader I know want to solve these issues so we can have dynamic worship experiences. Many of us go to conferences, read books, and study other churches to try to get to that one thing that will push us into a season of fully-engaged worship. If someone would just bottle that and give it to you, wouldn't you drink it? I know I would!

But this book is not just about one thing. It's about seven things to help you engage your team and your church in a worshipful way that cannot help but change everyone involved. I want to make you a promise: if you will take seriously these seven ideals, live them out, and work hard to instill them into the team you lead or on which you serve, you will experience radical growth in your personal and church-wide worship expressions.

The radical worship solution is not about how to play a more awesome guitar solo or get the right colors of lights on stage. It's about how we live and relate to one another. It's that simple. And that's radical.

Common Language

Before we discuss the seven ideals, we should make sure we understand the same words. Unfortunately, we have allowed some bad language to enter the church. We are not talking about your typical profanity or dirty jokes here, although in working with teams in more than a hundred churches, I have certainly heard some foul language and off-color humor! (By the way, did you hear the one about the . . . wait . . . what?) That sort of common language may be book worthy, but it's not what we are talking about here.

The reality is that too often we use good words in the wrong way. A few years ago as I was helping a band in a new church, one of the musicians consistently posted statements on Facebook that were foul and filled with less-than-honoring comments about people. The pastor approached him about it and suggested he dial back his choice of words and attitudes. The musician listened carefully and then said, "I don't understand why this is a big deal. I'm just the drummer. It's not like I'm the worship leader."

The fact is, indeed, it is a big deal—because as Christians we honor others as we strive to become more Christlike. But beyond that was his misunderstanding of what is - and who is - a worship leader.

Let's look at two common misused terms (worship leader and volunteer) and what each really means.

Worship Leader. The first piece of language we need to be clear about is the phrase *worship leader*. Churches have commonly used that phrase since the early 1990s. What do they typically mean?

A singer. A good singer. A good singer with a microphone. A good singer with a microphone and a guitar or keyboard. A good singer with a microphone and a guitar or keyboard who talks to the congregation between songs. A good singer with a microphone and a guitar or keyboard who talks to the congregation between songs and who *hopefully* is young with cool hair, skinny jeans, and please-oh-please-Jesus-send-us-one-with-a-tattoo!

Obviously finding talented leaders who know how to relate to people in all walks of life is important. That is not the point. The point is the language: how we define *worship leader*.

When I was a kid, many of the experienced church people called the Sunday service a "preaching" service. Or actually it was the "preachin'" service. You have to say that with a really thick Texas accent, as in, "Hey boys, let's go down to the church house and see the preachin' service."

Then later the pendulum swung to calling it a "worship" service and the music portion of the service became more important. So they needed a name for the leader of that part of the service just as they had a name for the leader of the preaching half (the preacher). You get the idea.

But calling one person the worship leader basically relegates everyone else to background singers with a karaoke track. We would never call them that, but that is what we are in essence saying.

Using this singular "worship leader" language for one person leads to some unwanted consequences. Just as the example of the drummer in the story above shows, people do not own the outcome when they are a background person. If the service is less than engaging, or people do not come to faith or change their ways, they believe it really has nothing to do with them—it is not their issue. They are not the *leader*. They also do not typically come as prepared because the bulk of the preparation is supposed to be done by the *leader*. They let their personal devotional life slide from time to time because the real spiritual impact of the service is based on the spirituality of the *leader*. Finally, the team is harder to hold together because it is the *leader's* team, not *their* team.

But let's all use the same definition here: *everyone* on the team is a worship leader: the drummer, guitar player, actor, singer, preacher, announcement giver, technologist, greeter, keyboardist, even the bass player! Each person has a shared and equal responsibility to do the only two things that worship leaders really do in a service:

Go to God and take others with you.

Did you catch that? We all have a shared and equal responsibility. Our roles are all different—just like the body of Christ (see 1 Corinthians 12:12–26). Some sing, some play an instrument, some act, some dance, some paint, some preach, some greet, some run sound, some put words on a screen, and some let people know what is coming next. But the responsibility to go to God and take others with us is shared and equal. The point leader (with the microphone) is important, but no more important than the drummer. (You are welcome, drummers!)

Here's a small exercise to try. Say this out loud: "I am a worship leader." Now say it with gusto: "I AM A WORSHIP LEADER!"

If you are a main ministry team leader, make sure everyone believes this in his or her core.

And if you are not the main ministry team leader, you believe this to your core.

When this happens—when everyone on the team embraces this truth—then you'll see everything on your team start to change. When we all equally own the goal of going to God and taking others with us, we are more prepared, we try harder, we pray more, and we care a lot more deeply about God's movement in our services. And, oh yeah, we stick to the church and the team better and longer.

Volunteer. This church conversation is way too common:

> ME: Hi person.
>
> PERSON: Hi.
>
> ME: What do you do in your church?
>
> PERSON: I sing.
>
> ME: Oh cool, are you on paid staff?
>
> PERSON: No, I'm just a *volunteer*.
>
> ME: (*pause*) What?

Here is another language problem. Your church has both paid and unpaid people. That is the nature of how most churches and some businesses are managed. Which one are you?

Notice I did not use the words *staff* and *volunteer*.

If you get paid for what you do, God has gifted you. God has opened a door of opportunity. God has called you to do what you are doing.

If you are not paid for what you do (and I have worked with hundreds of you), God has gifted you. God has opened a door of opportunity. God has called you to do what you are doing.

I have been both and can state with great authority that those true statements are exactly the same. Your role is just different. Do not take ministry less seriously because you are not paid. You have been called to do what you do just as the paid person has. Do the best you can. You have a lot to offer God, so offer it fully! Realize that if God has called you to do something, you should do it as if you are working for God, not for people (Ephesians 6:7). We'll discuss this idea more in-depth in the next chapter.

Now you might be thinking that you are not "called," you are just filling a role because it needs to be done. I understand that. Once when I was serving in a church plant, they asked for someone to work with the children. I was eager to help out. When I arrived, I discovered there were more than twenty children, including babies up through fifth graders. Frustrated at myself for having such zeal to serve and with a great degree of panic, I quietly helped with crafts, controlled the crowd, and looked at my watch every twentieth second, hoping the hour would go by more quickly. The preacher was really on a roll that night, because the next forty-five minutes passed like a snail in molasses. When it was finally over, I couldn't get to my car fast enough! I served and did the best I could. But I was never called to that ministry.

A few weeks later they again asked for helpers in the children's ministry. Did I eagerly get up and serve? Nope! Forget it! I was still recovering from the previous experience. In the meantime I had found the ministry to which God was calling me: playing guitar and singing.

I loved it. I worked hard at it. Even though I wasn't paid, I gave it my all as if I were. I was not a volunteer. I was a guy whom Jesus called to serve. That makes me a servant...not a volunteer.

Jesus has called you to serve. You are in your church, serving on your team at this moment because God wants you to serve Him at your church, on your team at this moment. You are not simply volunteering. You are obediently serving Christ. With that spirit and understanding as you read this book, you and your team will not just willingly volunteer, but will passionately serve.

The Symptoms

The script in the first chapter highlights a directionless team that is riddled with dysfunction. When we deal with people like that who exhibit similar demeanors, we can always see symptoms of bigger, underlying problems. Have you ever noticed anything like the following on your team?

* Isolationism: team members keep to themselves without really connecting with the rest of the group.
* Mission drift: team members hold different visions for the ministry.
* Competition: team members vie for roles or positions.
* Arguments: petty disagreements that could potentially lead to a cold war between members.
* Stereotypes: team members relate to one another based on roles and talents instead of who they are as a person.
* Mediocrity: the team does not improve.
* Effortlessness: team members are not trying.

* Boring services: worship gatherings becoming rote and predictable.
* Boring practices: rehearsals feel like work.
* Shrinking teams: bands, drama, and tech teams lose people.
* Pride: team members look out for themselves more than they do for others.
* Envy: team members wish they had someone else's gifts or talents.
* Surface relationships: the team doesn't really know each other.
* Internal focus: the team lacks fervor for reaching far-from-God people.

You and I both have lived through some, if not all, of these experiences. The question is, what do we do about it?

The Solution

When my friend Ben was in high school, he got a job as a delivery boy for a Chinese food restaurant. Although he wasn't crazy about it, he worked hard to earn his salary and tips. Each day he would pick up the little boxes of noodles, rice, main dishes, and egg rolls and deliver them to the customers throughout his hometown of Houston. Then he would drive back to the restaurant to get another load.

One afternoon, Ben loaded his car's backseat with several orders and headed out. To get to his first drop-off, he needed to get on the freeway, which happened to be under construction. (If you live in Houston, you know its freeways are always under construction). What Ben didn't notice were the cones that were constricting the freeway down from five lanes to four, then to three, and finally down to two.

By the time Ben noticed that he needed to merge, another car had pinned him in. Because of his speed, he had no choice but to slam on his brakes and plow through the cones. Just beyond the cones was a work zone where a section of the highway was cut out. His car went into the cut-out section, dropped two feet, and slammed into a tractor. Rice, Kung Pao chicken, and chow mein flew from the back of his car and splattered all over the inside of his windshield.

Ben was startled but okay. He learned a simple but valuable lesson that day—one that we will discuss throughout the rest of this book: pay attention to the cones and stay inside the lanes! I told you it was simple. The cones are there to protect us and keep us headed toward our goals. We will never get where we desire or are called—individually or as a team—unless we remain alert and stay on the road that leads directly toward those goals. In leading worship, as mentioned earlier, our shared goals are to go to God and take others with us. It's pretty simple, and there are cones that keep us headed that way.

The radical worship solution is to know what the cones are and how to stay inside them at all times. There is a way forward that will maximize your team's potential and keep them headed in the same direction.

Through my work with Worship Catalyst, the biggest issue I've found with bands, choirs, drama, tech, and other teams is that they have a hard time staying on the road toward shared goals. (Many times they don't even have a clear idea of what the goals are!)

This lack of clarity on goals was never more evident than in a one-year-old church that called me to help them clean up a mess. The pastor, Tim, explained to me that he and the worship leaders had some disagreements over philosophy and direction. This conflict had led to half of the band leaving the church, including the point leaders. They were extremely talented and well equipped to lead, but the division ruined what could have been something great. The remaining team members were disillusioned, confused, frustrated, and on the brink of quitting. Several of their friends had already left the church and most of them wondered if they should do the same.

I entered into this situation carefully, but with confidence that things could turn around. We found a new leader, cleared up the goal disagreements, held auditions to add new people to the team, and then started teaching and implementing a few team boundaries that we will discuss in this book. Within a few short months things were turning around. The team size doubled, forgiveness was offered and received, and one of the best signs of all, people were laughing and having fun again.

In the coming chapters, I will define boundaries, which we call values. We have implemented these in dozens of teams, and they will help keep you on the road toward your goal.

The Values

This book will explain why these boundaries, which we cannot cross for any reason, are excellence, creativity, unity, humility, authenticity, evangelism, and party. You will also receive tools to see how deeply these values are rooted into your team and suggestions on how you can rivet them in even stronger. Finally, I've included discussion questions called "What About Us?" at the end of each chapter to help your team process these values together.

The beautiful aspect of these values is they aren't restricted only to worship teams. Any creative team in any size church can apply them. In reality, these values are for every team in any field who wants to move forward together toward their goals. As you study them, apply them not only to yourself and your church team, but also to your family, your career, and your community.

Imagine being a part of a fully prepared, connected, and united team standing on a platform in a church and leading people toward Jesus. As you look out at the crowd, you see the congregation is not made up of observers, but of people who are engaged in a meaningful dialogue with God as they sing and participate in the worship gathering. There is power in that moment. Lives are changed, hearts are yielded to God, and when they leave, they take that experience with them everywhere they go. The worship gathering becomes a catalyst for a new way to live. Is this your church service?

It can be.

It should be.

It will be.

Let this map guide you to a radical worship solution and watch God ignite the heart of your team—and in doing so, He will ignite the heart of your church.

***

What About Us?

1. Have you ever been on a team with someone who resembles one of the characters from the first chapter? If so, what impact did that person have on the team?

2. In what ways did it affect your enthusiasm and willingness to connect with the team and its mission?

3. As you consider the list of symptoms, honestly assess each one and list those you or your team struggle with. Why do you think your team is a breeding ground for those symptoms to exhibit themselves?

4. How does understanding that you are a worship leader change the way you approach your role in worship? .

CHAPTER 3
Excellence: Doing The Best You Can With What You Have

I remember it as if it were yesterday . . .

(squiggly screen flashback scene)

It was the mid '90s. My hair was parted in the middle and feathered back. I wore awesome tennis shoes and khakis. My pastor had presented me, a young, green worship leader, with a captivating vision: we were going to the Holy Land. That's right: South Barrington, Illinois. More specifically, to a Willow Creek church conference. We could feel the excitement build just talking about it.

The day came and we pulled into the Mall of America-sized parking lot. The church building seemed to go on forever. Walking toward the front doors, I wasn't sure if I should be excited or overwhelmed by the sheer size and spectacle of everything. In comparison, I felt ordinary and small.

As we walked through one of the many sets of double doors and into the million-seat auditorium, something like a cloud descended over the room. For a moment, I wondered if that was the Holy Spirit. (It was actually haze . . . from a hazer.) I listened to the perfectly selected music as I looked out the floor-to-ceiling windows at the perfect lake nestled close by. All of a sudden a flock of Canada geese flew in and landed perfectly on the water, making a lovely rippling effect that seemed to move to the worship music now playing. I wondered if the church had bought the geese and trained them to fly around and sit on the lake to the tempo. I searched the program notes for a staff member called "Goose Trainer."

For the next three days I sat mesmerized in my comfy, padded theater chair. I experienced actors, who could have been on Broadway or in Hollywood (and, indeed, some actually had), who made me laugh and cry almost simultaneously. I heard a band play songs about Jesus with such precision that it was hard to tell if they were live or a recording. And the sound system! I could *feel*—not just hear—every note. I watched dancers and painters on the stage and on jumbo video screens. I was even enthralled with the guy whose only job was to take the pulpit on and off the stage. I rejoiced over the video of hundreds of people being baptized in the Geese Lake and sharing story after story of life change.

Clearly, each second of each element of each day was precisely thought through. The Willow team devoured every moment, turned each inside out, and looked at everything from every angle, as if to say, *How can we utilize this second to paint a picture of Jesus that will draw people to Him?*

In the middle of all this beauty, I sat with mixed emotions. On the one hand I was enraptured and thankful for the experience. During some moments it seemed as if I had touched the face of God. The only appropriate thing for me to feel was gratitude.

On the other hand, I experienced a deeper emotion. The emotion sounds something like, "Awww Maaan!" An *Awww Maaan*! feeling usually comes over us when something happens to take us by surprise—and not in a good way.

What brought on the "Awww Maaan!" moment was that I saw something that was absolutely unattainable. As I looked at all that was in front of me, I realized that if I worked hard my whole life, I would never see anything like this come to pass at *my* church. *My* church was a small country church in the middle of nowhere. We had cows grazing in the pasture next to the building. We had a cemetery behind the church, and across the street the corn grew so high that you had to stand in the church parking lot before you could even see the place. We were surrounded by corn, cows, and caskets. And that was the best part!

On the inside we had a little sanctuary with nine-foot ceilings. Our "advanced" lighting system was controlled by a switch on the wall. If you pushed the switch up, the lights came on, and if you pushed down, the lights turned off. The carpet, pews, stained glass, and hymnbooks, as well as the curtains that covered the baptistry were all red. Unfortunately, they were each a different shade of red.

Our piano player was a seventy-year-old woman who lacked rhythm. The organist was even older and he couldn't feel his left leg so he played random notes during prayers. Twelve people made up the choir—most of them tone deaf.

On the occasional times we had baptisms, we'd have to clean out the mice before we let people in the water.

So there I sat at the Christian "Mecca" that is Willow Creek church, comparing its excellence to my church that I felt was anything but.

My "Awww Maaan!" moment came from a place of intense desire to succeed. I wanted to help people connect with Jesus. I wanted our church to be a place known for its exceptionalism and creativity. I wanted to paint a beautiful picture of God. But the long, seemingly impossible road from here to there was crowding out those desires and dreams. It felt as though someone had just said to me, "Hey, man, land someone on the moon with no budget, staff, or resources. Oh, and do it by next Sunday."

We finally headed back home, and over the next few days I kept thinking about our experience in Illinois. I wondered, *What am I supposed to do with what I felt there? And how can I reconcile it with the reality of my church?*

And then it hit me: excellence is doing the best I can with what I have. It's not so much about *what* I have; it's about what I *do* with what I have. That realization emboldened me.

Maybe we can do something, I thought. So the ministry team and I brainstormed and began to add things to the services. We started small and added only one thing—a keyboard player to play different sounds—and then slowly we added something else and then something else, focusing on using the God-given talents of the people we had.

The True Meaning of Excellence

Armed with this new way of seeing excellence, over the next few years, and in more than one church, our teams grew and got better. We added drama and technology, dance and painting, great bands and video. In and of themselves, these things are not defined as excellence, no matter how good they are. But for us, we used and maximized the talents and resources we had. We weren't Willow Creek. We weren't supposed to be.

I've found that many church leaders get confused about true excellence. They push to ensure that the band is better, the lights are brighter, the sermon is stronger, and the customer service is friendlier—so they can reach more people and beat other churches. They work as though everything they do must be "excellent"—to the point that overshadows everything else in ministry.

That's not excellence. That's—to quote one conference speaker I heard recently—idolatry. Excellence is not a church race. Nor is it perfectionism. It is not putting on a show. It is not cutting edge. It is not for the purpose of being attractive. It is not to feed our egos. Excellence is not only for the most talented. It is not reserved for the megachurch. Bigger and technically awesome does not equal excellence. It is not something that wears us out or disillusions us from church.

Excellence, in its simplest form, is doing the best you can with what you have. That's it. Nothing more, nothing less. If the pursuit of excellence has ever burned you out, left you out, or caused you to lose relationships, you weren't pursuing excellence. You see, excellence is a spiritual thing. It is a response to God. It is worship.

I've seen excellence at Willow Creek, I've seen it in the smallest, most hick church around, and I've seen it at churches in between.

For instance, three years ago in the small, suburban-Tucson, Arizona, town of Marana, two guys started a church with a huge vision and almost nothing else. They invited me to lunch one day, and with incredible humility confessed that they needed help with music, room usage, technology, and personnel. I lent the support of the Tucson Worship Catalyst team, who jumped in and helped, providing musicians, singers, sound equipment, and people to train the team they were assembling.

Eventually we were able to help them build a full band and get them on their way in a healthy manner. Through hard work and persistence, the church took root and began reaching more and more people who were previously far from God.

A few months ago I attended a service there. The signs leading up to the church were clean and inviting, clearly identifying where I should go. Before I even entered the building, someone greeted me with a genuine smile and a warm handshake. Just inside the main door, I saw a welcome area with more friendly faces and clear directions for where I should drop off my daughter.

After getting her settled in her class—where I witnessed the teacher build immediate rapport—I headed back into the main worship space (a school cafetorium) and sat in a blue plastic chair. As people entered and found their seats, I noticed that upbeat popular music was playing through the speakers and an inviting welcome video was on the screen. I looked toward the back of the room where the tech "station" was and saw teenagers fully engaged in what they were doing.

Soon three teenagers, a businessman, and one of the pastors' wives stepped onto the small stage and began to lead us in worship. None of them were experts, but they were excellent! By hard work and dedication to God, they squeezed every bit of talent out of themselves and helped me experience Jesus in a way I had not experienced Him in quite some time.

The rest of the service was handled with just as much care and attention to details. These guys were not amazing at anything they did. They were better than that; they were excellent!

If excellence is not about pure quality of something, but a matter of effort and heart (doing the best you can with what you have), then an under-resourced church in the middle of nowhere can actually be as excellent, *or even more so*, than a big, staff-heavy megachurch. It's true: you can be excellent . . . even without geese.

Pursuing Excellence

Perhaps we need further motivation to drive for excellence. As we pursue it, we find that it is more than just a concept of hard work.

1. Pursuing excellence is spiritual.

I got my first real job when I was nine years old. I worked every day after school and most Saturdays at a drugstore where I served soft drinks and ice cream from an old-fashioned soda fountain. Over the three years I worked there, before I took an early retirement package, I was asked . . . um . . . told to do many things. I painted a hat rack, swept the sidewalk, took out the trash, and even washed my boss's car. For a while I did the job gladly, because I was compensated well: $1.25 per hour! Plus I got free supplies of all the Dr. Pepper I could drink and all the candy I could eat.

As the months and years went by, however, I began to feel used. What used to sound like gentle requests now rang in my ears as angry demands. My boss's tone became sharp and his language demeaning. Over time I became disenchanted with the job and I was glad when my junior high football schedule forced me into the aforementioned retirement.

In year one of that job I took pride in everything I did. By year three, I was doing just enough to get by. The way I felt about my boss (or master) defined the way I worked.

We all have masters. Consider the apostle Paul's words. While in prison, Paul wrote to the church in Colossae about how believers should live as followers of Jesus. He discussed their roles as wives, husbands, and children, and then he addressed slaves. In regards to these relationships, he wrote that we should "work willingly at whatever you do, as though you were working for the Lord rather than for people" (Colossians 3:23 NLT). Then verse 24 says, "Remember . . . that the master you are serving is Christ." When we do something our earthly master or boss is telling us to do, we are actually, literally, doing that thing for God.

Had I known about this passage—or should I say, had I cared about this passage—at age eleven, I would have done my job with more excellence. I would have swept as well as I possibly could. I would have painted with diligence and care. I would have actually used soap when washing my boss's car.

We are not called to excellence simply in our professional work, but in everything we do. We all have someone under whom we have submitted our lives and talents. For those of us who are church artists, singers, actors, dancers, musicians, and technologists, we submit to our pastors, worship ministry leaders, or creative arts directors. We offer our talent to God and to the church as a way of worshiping Jesus. In essence, we have become slaves to them. If this is the case, Paul wants us to realize our work is not for human recognition, but rather for God's glory. We are to serve and work as if Jesus is our direct boss.

That puts a different spin on our service at church. We serve Christ when we prepare. We serve Christ when we show up on time. We serve Christ when we come to rehearsal ready. We serve Christ when we memorize our music. We serve Christ when we attend lessons to get better. In Romans, Paul continues the idea as he pleads for us to offer up our bodies to Him as living sacrifices in response to His mercy:

> I urge you, brothers and sisters, in view of [in response to] God's mercy, to offer your bodies as a living sacrifice, holy and pleasing to God—this is your true and proper worship. (Romans 12:1 NIV)

We offer our minds, hands, feet, voices, arms, hearts, ears, spleens, and everything else to Him. All of it is His. I have nothing of my own. We are stewards and we give it all back to be used by Him for His glory.

The best way to cool off on a hot summer day in central Texas is to grab an inner tube and float down a river. When I was seven years old, my family and I were doing just that one day when

I got into a circular water current that my little seven-year-old arms could not handle. My tube flipped and I was pushed under the water and into a swirling part of the stream. I was stuck going 'round and 'round and I couldn't get up to the surface. Although my dad was paddling like mad to reach me, he couldn't. Eventually, a man saw my struggle, made his way over, reached down, and pulled me up to safety. I gulped a huge, deep breath, looked at the man, and then waited for him to do something nice so I could thank him.

What? Of course not! My dad and I both thanked the man incessantly and vowed to do anything to repay him for saving my life. It was our natural response to be full of gratitude and offer the man anything . . . everything.

God's mercy is rich. The Scriptures say it is new every morning (see Lamentations 3:23). We were dead in our transgression and sin until His mercy and grace saved us. It was not easy for Jesus to offer Himself completely for us. Blood, pain, ridicule, and immense spiritual struggle were involved. In Romans 12:1 Paul writes that when we see God's mercy, we give everything to Him *as a response.* This is our spiritual act of worship: to give everything away to the One who gave us everything in the first place. This is not over-the-top or exceptional. It's just reasonable.

When we practice, we practice as a response to God's mercy. Our hands and voice are His. When we try harder, it is in response to God's mercy. When we memorize, it is in response to God's mercy.

This applies to all areas of our lives. The way we build up and honor our spouse is a response to God's mercy. The quality and quantity of time we spend with our children is a response to God's mercy. Our spiritual leadership at home is a response to God's mercy. The way we spend money is a response to God's mercy. The purity of our dating relationships is a response to God's mercy. Our dedication at work is a response to God's mercy. The honor and respect we pay to our coworkers—even that is a response to God's mercy.

You see, when we start to see excellence for what it really is—doing the best we can with what we have—and we offer everything we have to God in response to all that He has done for us, we start to understand that excellence is not as much of a physical thing as it is a spiritual thing. We do the best we can individually and as a team because of Jesus' mercy. God sent the best; He deserves our best.

2. Pursuing excellence is relational.

Several years ago a young, talented guitar player joined our worship team. She breezed through our makeshift audition process, and we were thrilled to have her. She was ahead of many of the people on the team and helped strengthen us as a band.

She played a yellow guitar, and it sat on a guitar stand in the middle of the worship center platform all week, every week. It never moved except when she showed up for rehearsal. At the end of the evening, it went back to its lonely home in the middle of an empty stage until the next time we played together.

She had no second guitar at home. She gave no thought of improving her craft or putting in extra time to prepare for services. And so when other team members showed up ready and prepped to play, she wasted time muddling through, often playing in a style that was foreign to the song. She didn't even take the time to listen to the song before she arrived at practice.

She was letting her team down. She was letting God down. And ultimately, she lost her place in the group because she could not keep up with everyone else's rapid improvement.

This was tragically avoidable. Had she only offered her guitar-playing talent up to God as a living sacrifice, this story would have had a different ending.

The worst part was not that she lost her place on the team, but that she made a conscious decision to demonstrate her lack of commitment to a team that was trying to get better. The principle is that our team deserves our best. Excellence is not only spiritual; it is relational. We'll discuss this idea more later, but for now it is important to understand that when someone stands next to us in a moment or season of spiritual battle, we owe it to one another to be ready.

I was the quarterback on my high school football team. I wish I had a movie-worthy story about how our team overcame adversity to win the state championship, conquering our demons and fears. But our team wasn't that good. While we had a few moments of brilliance, mostly they were just sprinkled in among many more moments of sheer ugliness. One year in particular we had several layers of problems.

Our players were not particularly smart: many players bordered on ineligibility week after week. We were small: the left tackle (for the football novices, he's the one who guards the quarterback's blind side) was about 150 pounds with pads on. He was mean and tough, but really small. And the quarterback (me) was short: most of the time I couldn't see over the line to find a receiver.

But we had a bigger problem. We weren't prepared. The coaches spent plenty of practice hours with us and seemed to develop brilliant game plans to beat the opponents. The receivers consistently ran their patterns. The backs ran with diligence and knew where to go. The defense worked hard at their assignments. Most of the interior linemen were locked in and knew exactly what to do. But the team had one or two players who consistently missed their specific assignments—not because they had some physical challenge or a lack of effort during the games. They simply didn't put in the necessary work leading up to the game. The result was a quarterback getting sacked for more than 50 percent of the plays, runners having no place to run, and receivers getting zero opportunity to catch because the plays were never developed. In essence, the plays were doomed before they ever began because every person on the team hadn't worked hard to be prepared. Ten people could be ready, but that eleventh player's lack of readiness caused the whole team to lose.

Do you think that caused any relational strife?

Apply that to a church band, tech, or drama team. The guitar players, singers, and keyboardist are fully prepared when they come to practice. But the drummer doesn't know how the song starts so he asks to hear the song again. He stumbles through, making mistakes and causing the band to struggle. And everyone knows that one team member is not working as hard as the rest. The whole group sounds worse, people lose confidence, relational rifts begin, and ultimately, the team is not effective at its goal of going to God and taking others with them. It takes only one person not doing his or her best to hurt an entire team. When the stakes are sky high, we can't hide. Everyone knows when we aren't ready.

This is glaringly true in a drama ministry when everyone's lines, stage placement, expression, and energy are all based on the other people around them. An actor finds it difficult enough to memorize lines and honestly convey emotion, but when someone arrives unprepared, it causes the prepared actors to lose trust. This makes the team less effective.

This goes for sound engineers as well. They need to do their best with what they have too. Have you ever known a sound person to show up, make sure the system works, and then babysit the soundboard? Maybe they read a book or surfed the Internet during practice. Have you ever known that same sound person to miss a cue—maybe they didn't notice the guitar solo and never turned up that channel?

When this happens frustrations occur, confidence is lost, and the whole team suffers. Our whole mission suffers.

Whether we are a singer, dancer, technologist, actor, instrumentalist, preacher, or whatever we do, our fellow team members deserve our very best.

3. Pursuing excellence is communal.

It would be great to tell you that the following has happened only once, but unfortunately it has been repeated too many times for me to admit. After a rousing set of songs, the band sits down with the rest of the congregation to enjoy an awesome message. Five minutes into the message, mysteriously, the pastor can no longer be heard. What is it? Did he lose his voice all of a sudden?

His lips are still moving, so what could it be? It turns out the battery in his microphone is dead. It never got changed from the previous week . . . or from the week before that. The embarrassed sound engineer looks around to try and place blame on someone else who should have changed the batteries. The congregation turns around to look at the sound engineer who is on his knees now hiding from their glaring eyes. The pastor loses his focus and rambles a bit, until finally, someone takes the walk of shame from the back of the room to the front to either change out a battery or give the pastor a whole new microphone. I love it when that happens.

There are a few Scriptures that sometimes keep me up at night. One of them is Colossians 4:5–6: "Live wisely among those who are not believers, and make the most of every opportunity. Let your conversation be gracious and attractive so that you will have the right response for everyone." (NLT)

Are we trying to be excellent so we look cool and drive huge numbers into the service? Yes.

Umm . . . what?

Of course not. It is really important to have people show up. And since healthy things grow, we should naturally have more people showing up. But that alone is not a grand enough reason to be excellent. We always try to do our best because God deserves it, our teammates deserve it, and the people who show up at church deserve it. The people sitting in the seats might only pay attention to God for one hour out of the 168 hours in the week. And if they are typical church attenders, they aren't even going to be there every week. This means when they are there, finally paying attention to God, we need to deliver the best message we can, using everything with which God has equipped us.

If our sound system is humming or buzzing the entire time, it will distract people. If our guitar strings are out of tune or we are rhythmically or tonally all over the map, people won't be able to pay attention to the lyrics. If we stumble and bumble over our words as singers or actors, the message will not be clear. When it comes to our graphic engineers, I often say their job is the most important in the building. If people don't know the words and can't sing along or at least read along, they will feel out of place, confused, and stupid, and they will ultimately check out. If people only watch a great presentation and don't or can't connect with the Maker of the universe, we have given them the wrong thing. We will have potentially wasted an opportunity that might not come back around for a while . . . if ever. Make the most of every opportunity. *Be ready.*

Excellence Strives to Finish Strong

I'm what they call an 80-percenter. I fly through the first 80 percent of a project with great ease and joy. Energy and life flow through me as I work my way from conception to idea development to implementation. But when it comes to going that last bit and taking something from really good to amazing, I stall out. About 80 percent of the way through a project I often lose interest because I am 20 percent of my way through the next project.

Do you relate? Our bookshelves, filled with half-read books, stare at us as we celebrate our weaknesses. You see, it isn't a good thing when we don't finish strong. Since excellence demands that we do the best we can with what we have, we need to complete our ministry tasks with the same level of exceptionalism. For me, that means I need a finisher around me who loves looking at the final 20 percent of things and taking them from really good to great.

My wife is great at this. This book is an example. If you read my first drafts, you might not understand a thing. But she holds me accountable and helps me complete the mission for a strong ending.

We need people around us who complement our weaknesses. The last 20 percent is just as important as the first 80.

What Keeps Us from Finishing Strong

Many consider it a gift, a strength, or even something everyone should possess. I call it a cancer. It's perfectionism.

People do not ask for this disease and it cannot be attained by hard work. And yet those who have it commit to keeping it alive and well. They lie awake at night thinking about how they can take something that is amazing and make it perfect. Often their critical eye turns on others—and themselves—with judgment. They struggle to multitask and complete or move on to another project because the current project must be just right before they can finish it. If left unchecked perfectionists can alienate others because they will assume no one else's work will meet their standards. Ultimately they end up working alone.

It's like the person who stands in front of a brick wall polishing just one brick year after year while the other bricks get dirtier and dirtier. The one brick is amazing. The world is better for it and many lives are enriched by the shiny brick. But how much greater would the wall be if all the bricks received attention?

Much research on perfectionism has been done over the past twenty years. Jeff Szymanski, executive director of the Obsessive Compulsive Foundation, says that a key attribute of perfectionism is "contingent self-worth," the feeling that "in order to be a worthwhile person, I have to perform in such and such a manner, I have to behave perfectly."[1]

Self-aware perfectionists realize they must surround themselves with people whom they trust and who help keep their perfectionism in check.

How to Tell If It's Excellence or Perfectionism

I am often asked this question: "How do we determine if we are doing things with excellence versus crossing over into perfectionism?" The easiest way I can respond is to compare the two.

Excellence (doing the best we can with what we have) includes:

1. An unrelenting desire to offer God, our teammates, and the other people around us our very best because they deserve it.

2. A clear realization of the constraints with which we live. Everyone's "with what we have" is different.

Perfectionism looks like this:

1. An unrelenting desire to produce a great product that will cause people to realize we are good. Or a desire to produce a great product so we can feel good about what we accomplish. Ultimately it focuses on self rather than others.

2. An ignoring or rejection of the restraints we have. This can lead to frustration and anger.

Examining them side-by-side, it is easier to see our motives and set out on a better course for our team and us.

The Dangers of Being Just Good Enough

Do you remember Eddie, the worship leader from our opening story? He was a hard worker who seemed to want things to go a certain way. But did you notice he had given up on starting on time? In fact, when the new guy, Robert, showed up, Eddie let him know they were never prompt in their time management. By his own actions of plugging in cables as the rehearsal was supposed to begin, he reinforced the attitude that "just okay" was acceptable. Somewhere along the way, the group had settled into an attitude we call *Good Enough*.

Good Enough is common around church ministries. A team rehearses a song a few times and someone looks at his or her watch, realizing it's getting "late," and says, "Hey, I think that's good enough." The good intent is to honor each person's time. However, Good Enough assumes they can whip the song into shape on Sunday morning. Sometimes that works. Sometimes it doesn't.

Time restrains virtually every life and team. And that boundary means we must do the best we can with what we have. Sometimes what we have is not enough and quality is hindered while excellence is still attained. But we should always do the best to expand what we have so limitations are lifted over time. Extend practice by just fifteen minutes. Play the guitar for just ten more minutes several nights a week. Use driving time for listening to and examining new music.

Think of ways to raise the limits of *what you have so what you can do* is better.

No one embodies this concept more than my wife, Cami. For years, over multiple churches, she has cultivated drama talent. (I use the word *talent* loosely.) Sometimes the allure of being on stage and acting is so great that people without a lot of natural ability decide to give it a try. Many times I have meandered into a drama rehearsal and wondered why we don't have a more stringent audition process. I don't know much about acting, but I can tell these folks will not get an Oscar anytime soon.

But then the honing takes place.

Look that way.

Use this vocal inflection.

Walk over here.

Pause for 3.2 seconds.

Speak slowly.

Now speed it up.

And magically, in a limited period of time with limited natural ability, something really beautiful and good emerges. Cami and her team use every second. They always finish on time but with great efficiency. The actors are energized because they know their limitations were lifted a bit and they are emerging as good storytellers.

Many times I have watched this process and thought, *Okay, these guys are doing pretty well. Let's get out of here and get something to eat.* But Cami methodically, patiently, and graciously pushes, milking every bit of possibility out of a moment. Just one more time. Just a little more energy. Just one more step to the right or glance to the left. She isn't satisfied until they have achieved their best. It is not perfect. It isn't going to end up on Broadway. But it is excellent, and everyone sleeps well at night.

By the way, even after years of experience, Cami still spends hours preparing for rehearsals. Excellence is determined well before an actual rehearsal begins

Do not settle into Good Enough. Nudge the limitations. Expand what you do have and make it greater.

Measuring Excellence

How do you know when your team is living up to this value of excellence? How do you know you are on track and still headed toward the goal of going to God and taking others with you? One clear way will help you determine if you are sticking to this value: constant improvement.

Are you improving? Do you hear people sometimes say, "Wow, you guys are really getting better!" Are you having breakthroughs in the way the band sounds? Are harmonies tighter? Are dramas more engaging? Are the lights more focused? Is the tech team utilizing your technology to its full extent—to the point that they ask for better technology in order to raise the limits of what they can achieve?

If you said yes, you are probably doing the best you can with what you have, and you are being excellent.

However, if you are in a rut and things aren't improving in sound or lighting or music or anything else, you might have let this value slide. You are perilously close to detouring your goals of going to God and taking others with you.

You see, the natural result of us doing the best we can with what we have is that we get better and better. It is difficult to try hard at something and not improve. The saying goes, "Practice makes perfect." I have never seen this to be true, but I *have* seen that "practice makes better."

Raising the Value of Excellence on Your Team

There are some simple ways you can raise the excellence value.

Teach it. Remember that excellence is a spiritual issue; it deals with our personal relationship with Jesus. The Scriptures in this chapter are a good place to start describing that. As you have team devotion and Bible study times, make sure to include Romans 12:1, Colossians 4:5–6, and other Scriptures that deal with offering ourselves to God completely. I love discussing the life of Joseph, the Old Testament leader, and how he gave his all to God even in the worst of times. Ananias and Sapphira chose to give God less than their best while claiming they were giving it all to Him (see Acts 5:1–11). It did not end well for them.

You can also talk about people such as Venus and Serena Williams, who have been up hitting tennis balls at 6 a.m. since they were seven years old, or leaders like Jeffrey Immelt of GE who through hard work made his way from middle management to CEO over a nineteen-year period. You can find hundreds of stories like these. Success requires hard work. Constantly think of new examples of what excellence looks like in the Bible and in current life. Make it a regular part of your team's conversation. Also, a little honest self-analysis goes a long way. The questions at the end of this chapter will help with that.

Model it. Years ago, I mentored a worship leader who did not have a lot of natural talent. His singing was off-key and his instrument playing was rigid and suspect. Amazingly he was able to attract some really strong talent. Over time he got a good drummer, a couple of good singers, and a bass player. None of them were professional, but all were eager. Week after week for months I came to the practices and worked with the team, helping them learn songs and play them well. The drummer, bass player, and singers worked hard. But the worship leader was usually unprepared and clearly had not rehearsed during the week to get the most out of his ability. Over time, he lost every member of his team, except for his wife.

In working with dozens of worship leaders through Worship Catalyst, it is easy to draw a conclusion: the excellence of the leader drives the excellence of the team. If you are a team leader, be excellent. It starts at the top. Always do the best you can with what *you* have. If you have been slacking in some areas, just getting by, this would be a good time to change. If you are not the point leader, you can still influence others toward excellence by living up to it yourself.

Lift the limitations. If you've struggled with constraints that have stalled your capacity, think of ways to lift those limitations. Buy a new instrument. Extend practice a few minutes. Fix that broken speaker or raise some money to buy a new one.

Expect better from one another. Hold one another to a high standard. But it must flow from love. That chapter is coming soon.

Celebrate excellence. When someone is working hard, squeezing everything they can out of their ability, make sure everyone recognizes it. Draw attention to it, shining a light on this picture of excellence so others can and will start to shoot for it. You might think praising someone is counterproductive, elevating that person over others or, worse, over God. After all, we are just people taking others to Jesus. I would remind you, however, of Jesus praising the widow who gave her two coins (see Luke 21:1–4). He highlighted a person doing the right thing to teach a lesson about giving. We are wise to draw attention to biblical living so it becomes easier to see what we expect from our team members.

A Better Story

Now that we've discussed what excellence is and how we can pursue it, let's take another look at the book's opening drama. What if the band actually embodied excellence as a true value?

6:30 p.m. Worship Leader Eddie enters the worship center to prepare for band rehearsal. Sound Girl Maddie is already running cables and checking out channels.

Worship Leader Eddie: Hey, Maddie. You're here early.

Sound Girl Maddie: Yep. I got here a few minutes ago to get things ready. I can't stay, though, so Jimmy is coming to run the practice.

Worship Leader Eddie: Sound Jimmy or Janitor Jimmy?

Sound Girl Maddie: [*laughs*] Sound Jimmy. And since he's running practice, he'll do the service Sunday too.

Worship Leader Eddie: Are you okay with that?

Sound Girl Maddie: Absolutely. If I'm not at practice, I won't know what to look for.

Sound Jimmy enters.

Sound Jimmy: Hey guys.

Worship Leader Eddie and Sound Girl Maddie: Hey Jimmy!

Worship Leader Eddie: Thanks for being here tonight. Maddie says you're on for Sunday also.

Sound Jimmy: Yeah, I'll be there. And tonight I'll be back here tweaking and taking notes on the flow of the songs and solos and stuff like that.

Eddie's mouth drops slightly, a stunned look on his face. He looks around the stage, making sure things are in order; then he sets up his guitar, tunes it, and plays one of the rehearsal songs.

***

6:45 p.m. The rest of the band trickle in, talk to one another, and set up. When New Girl Taylor and New Guy Robert arrive, the rest of the band is already in place and setting up.

WORSHIP LEADER EDDIE: Taylor and Robert, let me introduce you guys to everybody.

Eddie makes introductions. People greet them. Maddie shows Robert and Taylor where to plug in and how to turn on the microphone. Eddie heads over to Guitar Kid Parker with some music.

GUITAR KID PARKER: I don't need it, man.

WORSHIP LEADER EDDIE: Did you get your printer fixed?

GUITAR KID PARKER: Naw, I think I have it memorized. I might need a little help on the bridge to the third song, but I'm pretty sure I have it.

Singers Suzie, Amy, and Taylor start working on some parts while the band finishes setting up.

***

6:55 p.m. Sound checks.

***

7:00 p.m. Worship Leader Eddie takes prayer requests and rehearsal begins.

***

What About Us?

1. Is the value of excellence deeply rooted into the DNA of your team?

2. What are you currently doing to get better at what you do?

3. Do you show up on time, having practiced before the rehearsal?

4. Have you ever said or thought, "That's good enough?"

5. [For the music team] Is the music in you or are you simply performing it, reading note by note or word by word? How is your memorization going?

6. [For the drama team] Are you becoming the person you are portraying or are you just memorizing the words, getting through the script?

7. [For the tech team] How are you preparing the sound, graphics, or lights during the week so the weekend experience is as good as it can be?

8. Who on you team is living out excellence? Who would you like to call out (as Jesus did with the widow and her offering) who elevates excellence as a value?

9. What is you next step in regard to living with excellence?

10. What is your team's next step toward living with excellence?

CHAPTER 4
Creativity: You Were Made for This

Trillions of snowflakes fall each year. God takes the time to make each one individual. Many believe that no two snowflakes are exactly the same.

Your body is made up of 7,000,000,000,000,000,000,000,000,000 (7 billion billion billion or 7 octillion) atoms.[1] The Milky Way galaxy, which houses Earth, holds a mere 200,000,000,000 (200 billion) stars.[2]

Scientists claim more than 8,000,000 (8 million) species of animals exist. Somewhere around 80 percent of them have yet to be found.[3] How many can you name? If you have the time, and you want to see some of God's more interesting creatures, Google the red-lipped batfish, the goblin shark, or (my favorite) the Venezuelan poodle moth.

More than 400,000 plant species have been identified—so far.[4] The mighty sequoia trees can grow more than thirty-seven stories tall and a staggering twenty-six feet in diameter.[5]

It takes 60,000 miles of blood vessels in your body to get the blood where it needs to be.[6] That means your blood vessels could circumnavigate the earth two-and-a-half times—although I wouldn't suggest you try that out.

More than 7,000,000,000 (7 billion) people live on the planet[7] and each person's DNA is different. Just like the snowflake, no two people are exactly the same.

We could go all day listing these amazing numbers. The reality is that in every aspect of nature—from oceans to deserts, sunrises to sunsets, gorges to mountains, and galaxies to microscopic organisms—the creativity of God is on full display.

Are You Creative?

I ask people if they are creative all the time. In seminars, conferences, and individual coaching sessions, the vast majority of people answer no. You might be thinking the same thing. In your mind is an image of a painter, sculptor, author, or virtuoso.

But here are two questions that drive the real answer to my question.

1. Who is the most creative being of all time?

2. In whose image were you made?

Both answers are found in the first chapter of the first book of the Bible. In Genesis 1:1 we learn that God is the creator of all: "In the beginning, God created . . ." A few verses later, after

God created the heavens and the earth, day and night, the sea and the land, the plants and the animals, He said, "Let us make human beings in our image, to be like us" (Genesis 1:26 NLT).

So doesn't it stand to reason that if God, in His very nature is creative, and we are made in His image, that we are therefore also creative? In fact, the more like God we become, the more creative we naturally become.

It is the nature of things to become more like their parents. Like it or not, you are slowly morphing into your mom or dad. Have you caught yourself saying something one of your parents would say? Have you looked in the mirror and jumped back a step because you saw one of them staring back at you? My dad told me a story once about the time he was putting on a jacket and noticed that out of the arm of this jacket emerged his dad's hand. Years later, the same thing happened to me! For a moment I was startled until I realized it was just my hand morphing into my dad's, just as his hand had morphed into his dad's. In the same way, we become more and more like God, our creator and Father, the closer we get to Him. That is our goal. In 1 Corinthians 11:1, Paul tells us that we should be imitators of him as he imitates Christ. If we act like Jesus, do the things He did, and live the way He lived, then we will become Christlike.

As we take more steps toward becoming like Christ, who is God, we naturally become more like Him. We have His image in us. And it is creative! In fact, if we are not exercising the creativity that is within us, we are living outside of our created purpose. This is why creativity is a value, a boundary outside of which our team cannot reach its goal of going to God and taking others with us.

You are creative! Be creative!

Creativity in Daily Life

What I am about to tell you is a little silly. In fact, it will probably make you laugh. Every morning I practice two things to help me stretch my creativity muscles.

1. *Toaster Strudel art.* One of my creative exercises is in how I get breakfast ready for Finley, my fifth-grade daughter. She loves Toaster Strudels. If you don't know what they are, a Toaster Strudel is a delivery method for healthy fruit and veggies. You basically take strawberries, cherries, or some other healthy fruit and you puree it. Then you add lots of a particular vegetable: high fructose corn syrup. But it's okay; it comes from corn! Once the mixture is ready, you squeeze it in the middle of a heavily-buttered (dairy) piece of flaky bread (grain). We like to believe that it's a compilation of all the food groups, a perfectly delectable and balanced breakfast.

Here's where the creativity comes into play. Along with each strudel comes a small packet of icing. (I'm still figuring out the nutritional value of the icing.) For too many Toaster Strudel makers, they hurriedly open the icing packet and squirt it haphazardly onto the strudel. But not me—I draw pictures.

I may not be a gifted artist (at all), but when I hold an icing packet in my hand, the world comes alive. Sometimes I draw people. On holidays I draw something seasonal. In the spring I create artistic numbers to count down the last few days of school. While I think it's a brilliant bit of genius, Finley needs a while to figure out what I've drawn. I think my mom is the only one who has ever appreciated my art.

This particular act of creativity is a challenge on several levels. For one, I am not good at it. For another, it happens early in the morning, and my creative juices don't wake up until at least 8 p.m. But even more difficult than the lack of natural gifting or the early morning hours is the fact that it has to happen daily. The first few months were easy, but soon I ran out of stick figures to draw and had to start really thinking.

As silly as this exercise is, it has enhanced my creativity in every area because it works a muscle that does not always get worked.

Creativity needs to be scheduled in or it will be the first thing to get scheduled out of a busy day. We all have deadlines and meetings, kids' activities, and household chores. Time speeds by and before you know it, the day is over and all we did was survive.

2. *Lunchbox notes*. The second thing I do in the morning to flex my creativity muscle is to write a note in Finley's lunchbox. It has to be different every day. My morning notes are like snowflakes: each with a unique way to say "I love you" or "Have a great day" or "Jesus is with you today." I'm often tempted to write a quick, standard greeting, but I know from experience that if I will take the time to write something new, I will have worked my creative muscles and Finley will have enjoyed a more personal and thoughtful side of me. When I start the day with creativity, it seems to jolt me into more inspiration in everything else I do all day long.

These are my exercises (feel free to steal them). But whatever you choose to do, *do something*. Find a few things you can do to build creativity into your schedule. Then, slowly, you will start to be more creative all day long.

What will you try? Writing a weekly blog? Painting a series of pictures? Driving to work a different way each day for a month? Pinning things on Pinterest every day? If you brainstorm, you can find hundreds of things to try. Challenge yourself to do it today—then be creative the next day and the next and the next.

Thankfully, we also experience moments of spontaneous creativity, when out of the blue the juices start to flow and something great happens. Seize those moments; they are a gift. A couple years ago as my daughter was taking her evening bath, I went in and sat on the toilet (lid closed, just to be clear) to have a conversation with her. We talked about how funny it was to sit on a toilet to have a conversation. A song idea started to emerge. I grabbed my guitar, returned to the toilet (closed lid), and we wrote a future hit called "Sitting on This Toilet." You will know it someday.

I have had several of those moments when a song or a new idea came out in a few minutes while driving or having a conversation with someone. As great as those moments are, we must not rely on them as our only pathway of creativity. That would be like a pastor who stands in front of a crowd to deliver a sermon week after week having not studied or practiced. Creativity is like a muscle that needs to be worked out consistently. In fact, the moments of spontaneous creativity are fostered by the hard work of a daily and weekly pattern of creativity.

What Holds Back Our Church Service Creativity

As I write this, my family is in transition. A few months ago we moved the headquarters of Worship Catalyst from Sahuarita, Arizona, to Las Vegas, Nevada. We, along with several other families, are also planting a church there. One of the benefits of this transition is that I have not had weekly worship leading responsibilities for a while. This has given us the opportunity to visit other churches in the area. We have been to small churches, big churches, old churches, blue churches . . . wait. Wrong poem.

I find it interesting how creativity plays out in each of these churches. Some of them have amazing imagination in their lighting and videos, song production, and sermon illustrations. Others have demonstrated ingenuity in the way they incorporate Scripture or make announcements.

Side note: most of these churches have the same "flow" in the service. This is for another book, but it applies to creativity. I have been the guest point worship leader for dozens of churches over the past few years. Typically, I will ask the lead pastor what the topic of the day is or how long the service runs—normal questions. What astounds me is how often the response starts with, "Here's how we do our services . . ." It does not matter what the pastor says after that. I have already learned that they do not engage their creativity muscles in how they plan services.

In most churches I visit, the order and flow is much like the next church and the next and the next! Two songs, greeting, prayer, two songs, sermon, closing song. Don't get me wrong; creativity happens in the context of this flow. But in the interest of congregational involvement and engagement, if you are in a position to speak into the design of a service, encourage the team to change things up! Find a new way. We have the greatest story ever told. We should find innovative and beautiful ways to tell that story. Is it *always* best to start with a song? Does that song *always* have to be upbeat? Does an upbeat song *always* communicate what you are trying to convey? Is it possible to use your creative potential to mix things up and engage people in a fresh way?

Worship leaders get caught in these boring ruts for three main reasons.

1. *Insecurity.* I had a friend who decided to shake things up one week by starting the service with imaginative Scripture reading, followed by a video, and then the message.

No songs before the sermon? But what if people come in late? They will miss the most important part! (Sarcasm alert.) It was just enough of a jolt to the congregation that they actually engaged and paid closer attention to everything that went on that day.

Unfortunately, the pastor did not feel confident because he was out of his rhythm. He mandated they go back to the "normal" way the next week. Sometimes insecurity blocks our ingenuity.

2. *Outside voices.* I wish you could have read emails with me the Monday after the first Sunday I used dancers to illustrate a biblical story. It turns out that dancing is not in the Bible. Did you know that? My team made the decision that Monday to fight for creatively telling the story of Jesus, even when a few loud voices fought against it. We should always listen to what people have to say, but we should never be governed solely by their convictions.

3. *Laziness.* The third and most prevalent reason we get into creative ruts is the hardest to overcome. A few years ago I was in the middle of a busy season traveling and training while trying to maintain a decent worship experience on the weekends. One day I heard myself say something to my team that tasted really bad when I said it: "We can plan a worship service in our sleep."

I was mailing it in, picking four songs, and hoping for the best. We have to be honest to deal with this one, and the core issue here is laziness, not busyness. Somewhere along the way we got really good at picking songs and decided that was our job. Don't get me wrong; picking the right song at the right place is critical and should be worked through carefully, but it is not the end of our ingenuity. When planning worship services gets easy, we have departed from this value of creativity.

Creativity Guidelines

There are a few guidelines when we talk about creativity. It might seem strange that we would need definable guidelines. In order to be truly creative, shouldn't we have ultimate freedom to do anything we want? Don't we need to think freely?

Ultimately, yes. But to reach that place of freethinking creativity, we need to get on a road that heads there. Oftentimes, creativity is not achieved because we do not have anything reining us in.

Here are the guidelines:

1. *Never say, "That's good enough."* This statement applies to excellence, creativity and every other value. We are doing

something immensely important so we should stop only when we get the right answer: the best creative idea for that particular moment.

2. *Do not be afraid to try something and fail.* In fact, if you fail, fail in a grand fashion.

One Christmas Eve, we thought it would be funny and intriguing to do a drama sketch involving characters in a live nativity scene. The wise man character (not the actor) in this sketch was drunk. He stumbled around the animals and other characters, making light of the story of Jesus and enduring the hours until he could go home and pass out. As the story went on, we realized how broken and sad the character was and how what he really needed was the baby who was in the manger next to him. It was meaningful and insightful . . . we thought. But several people got up and left. We did not analyze the audience properly, and looking back, Christmas Eve might not have been the best time to bring out an alcoholic wise man.

Another time we opened a youth camp with a mixture of live acting, video, intense music, and really long curtains hanging from the truss above. At one dramatic moment, all of the curtains were supposed to fall to the ground and signify that there was no more separation between God and us.

Tragically, only some of the curtains fell. More tragically, the one in the back that we were shooting video on fell only half way, leaving the closing part of the video looking distorted and weird. Most tragically, we effectively symbolized that there is indeed still some separation between God and humans.

We could go on all day discussing colossal fiascos in our creative history. But failure is good. In our failures we learned things such as knowing your audience and not shooting past your technical capabilities. The most important thing we learned, however, was realizing that we could still survive.

Fear destroys creativity. Do not be afraid to fail. My team has blazed a trail of glorious failure for you to follow. We survived a drunken wise man and a reconnection of the temple veil. And you will survive as well! Be creative. Try big. And when you fail, fail big!

3. *Don't immediately take the first good idea.* The better one is often right behind it. This takes discipline. Someone around the table might say something good, original, and meaningful, and the tendency is to stick to that idea before examining it further. However, if we take our time, we might just find that a better, more creative idea comes out next. As Jim Collins says, "Good can actually become the enemy of great."[8]

This brings up another sub-guideline: make sure you build in ample time for creativity. Inspiration does not often happen automatically. It typically takes time to process through an idea and make it into something great. That is why, as we said earlier, we must schedule creativity into our day and with our teams, or it will naturally get scheduled out. While we can do a lot individually to build those creative muscles, we also need to think about building the community's muscles. We can do this through planning meetings, projects, and worship services. One quick way to raise the bar is to make time for it. An inspiration might happen at any time. But the real investment in that inspiration, taking it from an idea to something great, will probably need a block of time. Be patient. Make space for creativity.

4. *Never say to a teammate, "That is a bad idea."* In our creative sessions, we have a strict rule that every idea is a good idea. If you were on our team and your idea was to have a hundred monkeys run out from the doors and congregate on stage after jumping on everyone's heads, we would greet that idea with, "Okay, let's put that on the board and talk about it."

Rejection is a huge imagination killer. Creativity feels like public nudity. We have this idea in our heads and we finally blurt it out. If that exposure is met with laughs or gawks, we will have a hard time ever revealing our ideas or ourselves again. However, if it is met with acceptance and honest dialogue, we will be more likely to keep trying to be resourceful. (It probably isn't best to try out the whole public nudity thing though!)

5. *Start the brainstorming as if money were no object.* I served on a team for a while with an amazingly gifted pragmatist. She was vigilant about making sure we were always within the bounds of our personnel, facility, and financial resources. This is a much-needed gift when dollars have to be stretched. But in the middle of the idea stage of creative development for a service, a marketing campaign, a video, or whatever, money and other resources need to be the furthest thing from our minds.

Back before I started listening to Taylor Swift (don't judge me), I overheard some college-aged worship leaders I was coaching talking about her 2009 performance at the ACM Awards. They were specifically talking about her singing in a rain wall. Not wanting to be left out of the conversation, I went to YouTube on my phone and watched it. Immediately my mind went to a few different ways we could use a rain wall in church.

A few months later we were talking about Easter and how the moment of Jesus' crucifixion until Sunday morning must have felt for His followers. It must have seemed like a nagging, horrible, incessant rain. As we talked, I realized, *This is the moment! Let's use a rain wall and have the pastor preach within it while he talks about how awful Saturday was, and then let's turn it off when Sunday comes. And let's utilize some good lighting to make the water come alive with different colors throughout the service to symbolize different things.*

When I shared those thoughts with the team, they jumped on it and took it from concept to great in just a couple hours.

Here is the highlight of that meeting: not one person ever said, "That sounds expensive" or "We don't have colored lights in the church" or "What do we know about building a rain wall?"

After the idea had solidified in our minds and we were getting really excited about it, someone finally said, "So does anybody here know how to build a rain wall?" We asked around and a couple people on our production team took it on as a project. It turns out you can find out how to do almost anything on YouTube. With some ingenuity and time, our team constructed a rain wall for Easter in a rented facility for less than $200. The effect was just what we needed to talk about Jesus, and many people gave their lives to Christ that day.

Open your mind. Assume anything is possible. Remove boundaries. Maybe your team will run into some walls that are too high, but maybe there are other ways to get over the wall.

You will never know until you try. The less you have, the more creative you get to be!

Micro-Creativity versus Macro-Creativity

Mr. Webster's Dictionary is not going to contain the words *micro-creativity* and *macro-creativity*, but we are going to discuss them anyway. Many people carry a misguided assumption that creativity is always obvious and blatant, like a painting or a rain wall. However, in my experience with churches and leaders, I've found that creativity is most often hidden. It is obvious and appreciated only to people who understand it. For instance, when was the last time you looked at one of Pablo Picasso's paintings? Were you amazed and transfixed by the imagination of the piece? Probably not. In fact, you most likely looked at it and wondered why in the world someone would pay 155 million dollars for one, which Steven A. Cohen did in 2013.[9]

If you looked at that particular piece, called *La Reve*, you would probably say something like, "I wouldn't have paid 155 *dollars* for that." The issue is not that Picasso wasn't creative. He was immensely innovative, co-inventing cubism, and moving art forward so much that he became the best-known artist of the 20th century. Most of us just don't get it.

Actors and musicians understand this also on a small scale. When a guitarist plays a lead line in a different way or an actor pauses or makes a facial expression that draws everyone in, the guitar players and actors in the crowd see it and are moved by it in some way. Everyone else enjoys it and gets to have a great experience. Most people don't know what just happened, but it was great. This is micro-creativity.

Subtle blue lights are added at just the right time. The band goes into a half-beat section changing the feel of the song. Instead of picking random images for backgrounds, the graphic artist uses images and film that describe the words being sung. A worship leader builds silence into a set of songs, allowing people to connect with God before moving on to the next piece. These are small things, maybe even unnoticeable to the untrained eye or ear. But they help people connect with Jesus.

Contrast that with macro-creativity: Changing the seating in the room. Painting a wall pink. Monkeys on stage. A painter or sculptor working on stage during a sermon. Even a rain wall running as people enter a room. It is obvious and bold. Everyone knows that something just happened. They might not "get" it, but they know it was different. In these bold leaps, sometimes people get up and leave—been there! Sometimes people complain to the pastor—been there! Sometimes you get an email you don't appreciate much—been there a lot!

Unless, of course, the culture is already set for creativity. For some churches the monkey thing would cause a church split. In others, people would be like, "Cool. Monkeys." The "monkeys are cool" church has been working on innovation for a while, so it's nothing new. The "church split" church has not seen anything fresh or artistic since the "new" fellowship hall was finished in 1978. People are still talking about that.

If you are a leader in a "church split" situation or have a pastor who struggles with the idea of innovation, then focus on micro-creativity. Play a song a little differently. Add a monologue into a service (not in biblical costume preferably—and *not* a drunk wise man). Change the lighting subtly to bring more focus to a moment. Have someone read Scripture during a song. We could go on and on with ideas, but the *big* idea is to add new things and change old things. Just do it in a way that does not immediately catch people off-guard. You will have time and space for that later after those around you are accustomed to change.

And then add monkeys.

Raising the Value of Creativity on Your Team

Hopefully we have been able to spell out why creativity, like excellence, is a spiritual issue. We must daily live it out personally and within our teams. Here are some ways to ensure we do just that.

1. *Teach this*: You were made in the image of God. God is creative. Therefore, you are creative. The more Christlike you become, the more creative you naturally become. If you are not living creatively, you are living outside of your created purpose. Creativity is a core and fundamental issue in a believer's life.

2. *Be creative.* As we have said, start small, but make sure you are always innovating. If you are the leader, plan some more time into your practices or meetings and make sure you personally create. Change the dynamics or the voicing, take one more pass at that presentation, or adjust the slides to reveal a little more meaning. You personally take on the responsibility of being the lead creator. If you are not the leader, practice micro-creativity

in everything you do. Find some small way to innovate and then discuss those things with the team.

3. *Build a team.* One of the greatest days of my life was when I said out loud, "If this whole worship planning thing comes down to my own personal ability, it is going to get really boring and stale quick!" It was a moment of humility and honesty where I realized I was the stumbling block to the future of our worship services. So I built a team to design services. I found the most creative people I knew, and we immediately raised the ceiling of our creativity. Since that day, I never plan services alone. Neither should you.

4. *Pursue every week.* Make it your goal that every week you and your team will try at least one new thing. This could be the way you play a song, a creative exercise, a new video or creative element in a service, or a way you express prayer or devotion in your team. If everyone sees the same thing every week, you actually demonstrate that creativity is not important.

My parents have used a phrase since I was a child: "He's a chip off the old block." They are saying that the child has become like the parent. The parent is the block and the child has the characteristics of the old block.

I am a singer. My daughter, Finley, is a singer. When she sings, I beam with pride. God is honored, like a proud parent, when you innovate and create things. You are a "chip off the old block." You have the characteristics of your Father. You are honoring and worshiping Him when you create.

***

What About Us?

1. Read Psalm 139:13–18. In what ways do you see the creativity of God in this passage?

2. Why do you think creativity is so important to God?

3. In what ways are you most creative?

4. When, or in what environment, do you feel most creative?

5. What are some next steps for you to become more creative?

6. Do you think your worship services are innovative?

7. In what ways could you and the team be more creative in the services?

8. How can you practice micro-creativity and macro-creativity in your worship environment?

CHAPTER 5
Unity: Always Fight for Peace

"My wife left me. It's over." My friend told me over the phone late one night.

A Saturday morning email from a ministry partner read, "Our son has shut us out of his life. We have no connection to our grandkids anymore."

Over lunch a family member revealed to me that her toxic work relationships had led to severe medical problems.

A devoted pastor ashamedly told me he was shutting down his new church. He just couldn't go on.

In each of these stories I tried my best to share life, give hope, and offer encouragement. But the brokenness in each of these lives shared something in common: disunity.

Disunity affects everything. The last story, about the church shutting down, was especially frustrating. A little more than a year before, the church had started out with energy and focus, determined to make an impact in their community. But over time they lost their clear mission: to go to God and take others with them.

All of the values we discuss in this book are equally important, but unity has a broader effect on all of them.

So until you get unity right, stop having worship services.

Stop singing. Stop playing instruments. Quit writing scripts and songs. Stop upgrading your equipment and changing out your choir robes.

We are wasting people's time and a lot of God's money on things that have absolutely no purpose if they are accomplished without unity on your team and among your leaders.

The Necessary Ingredients to Have Real Unity

While all the values we look at in this book and that we incorporate into our team ministry are of equal weight and importance, this particular value is the glue that holds all the others together. And as we will see, the consequences of this one value not being lived out seem to have a greater negative impact on our ultimate goal.

Hopefully, you have not been part of a church split. When churches break apart or die, I can guarantee you it isn't because the music was too loud. It was not the pastor's glitchy microphone. It wasn't "all those new songs." It was not the color of the carpet or the new pastor's ideas. It wasn't even a moral failure or sin. In almost every case, a church splits because people cannot get along.

You see, the enemy is at work and his desire is to steal, kill, and destroy you, your team, and your church (see John 10:10). And he knows that breaking up relationships is a good way to do that. A moral issue that crushes a spiritual leader and his or her ministry impact is awful. But it is the *relational response* that often becomes catastrophic.

For instance, a drummer struggling with an addiction is a fight the entire team takes on together until the darkness is forced back. When this happens, we win the battle and unity can be restored. But sometimes a fellow team member can become disillusioned and back away from the team because in his or her mind the addiction should have had consequences. A response like this is crippling to a ministry and takes away the joy of a battle won. When unity is affected, impact is lessened or even completely sidelined.

A couple years ago I had the opportunity to help a church in northeast United States. The plan was for me to work with the group for a day and a half, helping out with band practice sessions and offering seminar-style teaching. We started the day with an icebreaker time, just getting to know the various team members. Most of them were amicable and grateful for the work I was doing with them. One of them was not. He was a band member who we will call Bill.

In a short conversation with Bill, I found out that he had been part of the team for many years, even more than the pastor or worship leader. He let me know that he was the one who kept the band together during the last transition and that the biggest problem we needed to address that weekend was the sound.

In fact, he mentioned that the band was "just fine" and the sound system itself was really good (he had designed it and paid for it himself), but that I should spend all my time in the sound booth helping the sound guys learn how to mix. It seems that the awesome work the band was doing was being diminished by the inadequacies of the audio team. I thanked him for being there and moved on to another conversation.

The band played a song while I watched and listened. Bill was quiet, not connecting with any other band member. After a couple songs, I made a few comments about the way they played and offered some suggestions on how to make the songs better.

Instead of listening, Bill, who happened to be playing drums, spent the time working on tightening his cymbal stands and adjusting his music. Then when a good dialogue around my comments had begun among the team members, Bill finally spoke, interrupting the guitar player.

"It doesn't really matter what we play up here. The sound is so bad that people can't hear what we're trying to play anyway. It just sounds awful. The sound guys don't know what they're doing." Bill knew the sound guys were listening.

The results of this awkward moment were hurt feelings and frustration. Several people even admitted they no longer wanted to be on the team. It wasn't as if this was the beginning of the weirdness; bad feelings had been going around for a long time, but Bill's comment brought everything to the surface. What Bill did was sad and damaging. Clearly he did not understand biblical unity.

I decided right then that we would spend the better part of the next day searching the Bible together and discovering what it has to say about how we are to get along. What we discussed were the four amazing gifts God gives the church and how unity makes them possible.

1. God anoints us to do impossible things.

Psalm 133 says:

> How good and pleasant it is when God's people live together in unity! It is like precious oil poured on the head, running down on the beard, running down on Aaron's beard, down on the collar of his robe. It is as if the dew of Hermon were falling on Mount Zion. For there the Lord bestows his blessing, even life forevermore. (NIV)

Oil is anointing. Anointing in the Bible can be described as "God on flesh doing those things that flesh cannot do."[1] When God's people live together in true unity, they experience an anointing. Anointing is on people. The oil is *on* Aaron, the first high priest after God delivered the Hebrews from slavery in Egypt. Anointing is typically for a purpose—that someone who cannot accomplish something by himself or herself can do something amazing for God. When we pray for anointing, we do not just pray for some vague thing. We pray for God to empower people to lead, evangelize, pray, preach, or accomplish something they cannot do in and of themselves.

Therefore, it is imperative that God's anointing be on us when we worship. If all we are interested in is accomplishing the things we can do on our own, we are not going to get much done for the Kingdom. Our desire must be to see God do things through us that are impossible without Him. In fact, nothing we achieve on our own is all that valuable eternally anyway, so God's anointing is essential.

And without unity, we aren't anointed.

Unity is the context for God anointing His people. It is in that context that Aaron had a crazy amount of oil poured over him, his beard, and his robe. I love that it was messy. The anointing got all over him. It was not a small amount that was rubbed on his forehead. He was drenched.

When we find unity in our teams—true unity without bitterness, anger, envy, competition, irritation (should I go on?)—we also find that God anoints the service and ultimately people's lives.

I experienced this with our team in Arizona. I sometimes had a hard time finding someone to take the lead on a song because people kept giving it away to another team member. Our practices sometimes had long breaks where people were talking through real issues in each other's lives with deep concern for one another. The team members were not competitive with one another and they felt each other's pain. When we approached worshiping God in practice or with other people during church services, God's anointing had no barrier; it flowed into and through us to the congregation. This is what we desire: an anointing so great that we are not the only ones who experience it. It is lavish and messy and might even splash onto someone else.

Do you want church without anointing? Or do you want to accomplish impossible things for God? Of course the latter, but it requires the work of unity.

2. We show the world who Jesus is.

This is a great moment in the Bible: Jesus prays for us. He had been praying for His disciples and then He turned His prayer focus to the people who would believe in Him later—that is us!

My prayer is not for them alone. I pray also for those who will believe in me through their message, that all of them may be one, Father, just as you are in me and I am in you. May they also be in us so that the world may believe that you have sent me. I have given them the glory that you gave me, that they may be one as we are one—I in them and you in me—*so that* they may be brought to complete unity. Then the world will know that you sent me and have loved them even as you have loved me. (John 17:20–23, NIV, emphasis added)

This passage has an important two-word phrase in it: *so that.* In fact, you see it twice. It is a really important set of words because it points to motive, reason, or purpose. The question is not *if* Jesus wants us to live in unity. The question is *why* Jesus wants us to live in unity. The reason is so that the world may believe that God sent Jesus to bring us life. Unity as it relates to us is not just about us. It is also about those who do not know Jesus. Unity among believers is about evangelism.

In verse 22, Jesus prays, "I have given them the glory that you gave me..." *Glory* is one of those difficult-to-grasp words. A few Bible dictionaries say this about glory:

—divine power and majesty

—the weighty importance and shining majesty that accompany God's presence

—the glorious moral attributes, the infinite perfections of God

—everything that makes God beautiful and great[2]

It is a bit elusive to understand fully because we have never seen anything like glory before. The Bible itself does not even really expand that much on it. It just kind of says, *Hey, here is God and He's beautiful and amazing and shining and perfect and clearly in control, and we're going to wrap all of that up into a word and call it glory!*

God gave Jesus His glory. Jesus gave us that same glory so that we would be unified. But that was not the end of it.

Jesus is saying: Father, I have received divine power and majesty—weighty importance and shining majesty, glorious moral attributes, infinite perfections—from You. Now I am going to give that to these people and the others who will come after them *so that* they will have unity.

And then He prays, "Then the world will know that you sent me and have loved them even as you have loved me."

The end game for unity is evangelism. Jesus has God's glory to give us *so that* we will live in unity *so that* people will know Jesus. Unity is the context for far-from-God people to be able to come to know Jesus.

3. Clear the way for pure, acceptable worship.

All of us who worship are going to pay close attention to this one. The context for worship itself is unity. Paul tells us:

> May the God who gives endurance and encouragement give you the same attitude of mind toward each other that Christ Jesus had, *so that* with one mind and one voice you may glorify the God and Father of our Lord Jesus Christ. Accept one

another, then, just as Christ accepted you, in order to bring praise to God. (Romans 15:5–7, NIV, emphasis added)

There is that phrase again: *so that*. The apostle Paul is being clear here: unity is needed for worship. In fact, unity *is* worship. It is not possible for us to claim to be worshipers when we have bitterness against our neighbor or teammate.

Jesus takes this idea to a whole other level in Matthew 5:21–24. He is speaking in the Sermon on the Mount, in the section on the beatitudes—blessed this, blessed that, blessed the other. Then He discusses how we are salt and light. In my mind, Jesus then rolls up His sleeves and changes the subject—and his tone—drastically: "Now we're going to talk about murder!" I'm sure a hush fell over the crowd.

He starts by saying that if you are angry with someone, you are subject to judgment, as though you killed that person. Then He says if you call someone an idiot, you will go before the court. Then He drops the big bomb: "If you curse someone, you are in danger of the fires of hell" (NLT).

I can see the lights flicker and hear the orchestra sound—*dum, dum, dum*—and a bloodcurdling scream.

But then Jesus gets really practical. He says: So if you are presenting your sacrifice at the Temple and you suddenly remember that someone has something against you, leave your sacrifice there at the altar. Go and be reconciled to that person. Then come and offer your sacrifice to God (Matthew 5:23–24, NLT). This could not be any clearer. Do not worship God if you have a relational struggle going on.

You are offering a sacrifice to God: your voice, your instrument, your abilities. When you worship, you offer those things to God as a sacrifice to Him. But He is saying that if you have an issue with someone, do *not* offer your gift, your sacrifice—at least not now. Get the relationships fixed first. Literally.

I had a pastor once who was getting ready to offer his sacrifice of a sermon to God. Just moments before he was to speak, he realized there was something critically wrong between his wife and him. As the last song wound down, I noticed that he left his place on the first row of the church and walked back to where his wife was sitting halfway back in the sanctuary. He knelt beside her and spoke a few words with her. They embraced and then he made his way to the platform to preach.

Later I asked him what that was about. He told me he had been short with his bride that morning and it was hindering him from offering his full self to God in worship as he sang and then preached. What a great lesson! Do not get up to sing or play or act or preach or anything else that is your sacrifice unless the relationships around you are sound.

It is interesting that Jesus equates this relational adversity to murder. It makes me think of a busy Sunday morning in the church parking lot. People are rushing onto the lot, parking, and then rushing into the church. One particular person, new to the church, gets out of his car, and brandishing a knife, brutally murders the first person he sees. People see this happen. The man calmly puts his knife away and walks into the church to the front row where the music is already playing. With blood dripping down his hands and arms, this man raises his hands and sings with a full voice, "I surrender all."

What would you think about that person? Hypocrite? Liar? Insane? Dangerous? Unrepentant? Whatever we think of him, he is a murderer who is going through the motions of worship. I'm sure we would all say it isn't really possible for him to be genuine in his offering to God. And yet Jesus says that we are that man when we try to offer a sacrifice of worship to God while we harbor broken relationships. We are unrepentant murderers trying to offer God something He doesn't really want. "Leave the gift at the altar," He says. Don't offer it. Leave it there. Wait until the time is right and the relationships are sound, and then offer yourself completely to God.

Is it possible that God could really want us to refrain from worship? It depends on what we mean by worship. If we have a surrendered, repentant heart and unified relationships, we are already worshiping God. But if we offer some counterfeit worship, God is clear: don't do it.

In Isaiah 1:13 and 15 (NIV), God says, "Stop bringing meaningless offerings! Your incense is detestable to me. . . . I cannot bear your worthless assemblies. . . . When you spread out your hands in prayer, I hide my eyes from you." In verse 14, God says that their worship is "a burden to me."

It is clear that from God's perspective, He would rather us not meet than go through the motions. He repeats this idea in Amos 5:23 (NIV), where he says he will quit listening to our music. Those are great words from God to a worship leader! "Away with the noise of your songs! I will not listen to the music of your harps"[3] (or your electric guitars). Ugh!

The bottom line on unity and worship is this: God-honoring worship does not occur in the context of broken relationships.

We are living outside of our created purpose when we choose to leave severed dealings unmended. There are, of course, those instances when we work and work to fix a relationship and the other person will not budge. As we will see later in this chapter, we do not stop fighting for peace. However, we can come to a place of reconciliation in our hearts, even if the other person chooses to remain separate. This is not the norm. Typically we can get to a place of peace with anyone—and we must. The worship of God demands it.

4. We receive God's blessing.

In 1 Peter 3:8–9, the apostle tells us:

> All of you, be like-minded, be sympathetic, love one another, be compassionate and humble. Do not repay evil with evil or insult with insult. On the contrary, repay evil with blessing, because to this you were called so that you may inherit a blessing. (NIV)

The final component that we cannot live without in church is God's blessing. A quick web search of *blessing* finds several different definitions of the word. My favorite is Merriam-Webster's explanation: "Help and approval from God."

I mentioned previously that I played quarterback on my high school football team. Our biggest rival was a school that was about fifteen minutes from ours but in a completely different town. Each year leading up to the big game, rumors would fly about us prematurely burning the other school's bonfire or their guys finding and killing our mascot. It was brutal and made for great anticipation of what would take place on the field. The previous year, while they were ranked eighth in the state, we had humiliated them on their own field, taking away their dream of a state championship. Understandably they were still angry and wanted revenge on our turf. Our teams were both doing well and had a real chance to go deep into the playoffs. We were well coached, well conditioned and ready to win this grudge match for a second straight year. We took the field under those Friday night lights and kicked off at 8:00 p.m.

Three hours later I was back in the locker room having thrown four interceptions and having single-handedly and literally thrown the game away. Dejected, I slowly cleaned up and drove home only after everyone else who might want to talk to me had left. When I pulled into my home's driveway, I saw my dad sitting on the front porch. I sat across from him and waited for him to speak.

"Tough game."

"Yeah."

"You played well."

"You're crazy. I was horrible."

"Do you know how many passes you threw that were dropped? Do you know how many times you were knocked down in the backfield? Do you know how many bad calls the refs made?"

And for the next thirty minutes or so, my dad encouraged me. He helped me start to heal, and he let me know that no matter what, he approved of me. In other words, he blessed me.

Help and approval from anyone, especially a parent, is amazing. It helps us overcome and move on to stay strong in the face of difficult times. But what Peter says here is that God

Himself will bless us. He helps us and approves of us. All we have to do is bless others. Help others. Approve of others. Offer a helping hand and a gracious spirit to the people around us.

Your team and your church need God's help and approval. All of our churches and teams need that. We need His help to introduce people to Jesus and to stay focused on our shared mission. We strive for His approval, though, and like my dad's approval of me, His approval of us is not based on our performances.

As we see here, we receive God's blessing in the context of unity. Peter fully acknowledges that relationships are hard, filled with evil and insults. But he writes that if we bless others no matter what, we will receive God's blessing. We need that in our worship experiences and on our teams.

Anointing. Evangelism. Worship. Blessing.

Can we even imagine a church without those things? Would that even be called a church? These four ingredients to our worship experience are all gifts from God that come with His power for changing the world. They are all necessary for accomplishing what Jesus asks of us. They are all attainable. God is standing by to offer them freely to us and to our churches.

When I used to live in the humid climate of Houston, Texas, mold would sometimes grow aggressively on the sides of people's houses. Mold can grow only in a moist environment. Now that I live in the desert, mold has no chance. In the same way, anointing, evangelism, worship, and blessing can grow only in a unity-rich environment. We cannot control how much we receive of these things from God, but we can control the environment in which these vital components can grow. With all our hearts we desire God's anointing, exponential evangelism, heart-felt worship, and lavish blessing—and we can have these things. But often our activity actually works against them.

So how do we cultivate a unity-filled ecosystem where anointing, evangelism, worship, and blessing grow freely?

Fight for Peace

I was minding my own business, watching TV with my family, when I got a text. Against my better judgment I took a quick mental break from the show to read it.

> I AM DONE. NEVER PUT ME ON THE SAME TEAM WITH JIMMY AGAIN OR I CAN'T BE IN THE BAND.

Well, *that* TV show was over. I kept watching it with my eyes and tried to stay engaged to some degree for my family's sake, but my mind was racing as I slowly grew more frustrated and concerned. *How did we get from 0 to 100 so fast?* I wondered. *What did Jimmy do? Is there a moral issue involved? Why am I hearing about this at 10 p.m. on a Friday?*

All I knew was that Jimmy, an instrumentalist, was moody. In fact, he was sometimes so moody, he was mean. That was nothing new. We'd had multiple conversations about that.

I made the decision to go to bed without answering the text. I needed to sleep on it. I woke up Saturday morning to an email from a different person on the team saying the same thing: "Don't put me with Jimmy anymore. I can't handle him."

A phone call from a third person later in the day confirmed I had a real problem on my hands.

In Ephesians 4:1–4, Paul wrote that our biggest problems in ministry would be ourselves. He told the people in Ephesus, and us, that when we go out in ministry we should have humility, gentleness, patience, and the ability to bear with one another in love. This is a really different list from what I would typically think to give people!

At Worship Catalyst we help new churches develop strong worship leading teams. In talking with dozens of church-planting pastors through the years, a common question I receive is, "What do I need to succeed?" Early on I would say things like: money, strong leaders, energy, and an amazing lead guitar player! But Paul, who is a little smarter than I am, knew that the battle toward successful ministry was not going to be money or leadership or energy or even music. He knew that the real problem was going to be ourselves.

In verse 3, he wrote, "Make every effort to keep the unity of the Spirit through the bond of peace." (NIV) Make every effort. How many efforts is that? Every.

But when do I stop? When you run out of every.

But they don't want to reconcile. Make every effort.

But I don't really need them. Make every effort.

I think Paul was careful not to say, "Make ten efforts" or "Make effort until they don't respond."

But I sent a text, an email and tried to call. Make every effort. Don't stop.

The real issue here is not some sort of unity between you and someone else. The real issue is the unity of the Spirit. There is one body, one Spirit, one hope, one faith, one baptism, and one

God (see Ephesians 4:5-6). We are keeping the unity of the *Spirit*, not just the unity between you and me. It is not just for us.

There is a spiritual dynamic to unity. We should never quit fighting for peace. Ever. We don't have the right to be judgmental or bitter or even bored with one another. We are *one*. There is an interconnectedness within the body of Christ that many have lost somewhere along the way. It is not all about my family, my needs, my wants, or my time. Paul says it is not about *me*, but about *we*.

Armed with that understanding, I talked with each person who had told me they didn't want to be on Jimmy's team anymore. After fifteen or so minutes of sharing with them some of the details of Jimmy's life, they backed off, had compassion, and recommitted to work through the problems. They had not taken the time to know that someone very close to him had recently abandoned him. They did not know that sixty hours of work every week didn't provide enough to pay for rent and food. They did not know about the medical issues that affected the way Jimmy thought and acted. In other words, they did not know why Jimmy was the way he was. They just didn't like it.

Don't get me wrong, our crummy life experiences do not give us the right to be rude, demeaning, cold, short, or dismissive. Jimmy and I had many talks about that. In fact, those conversations got pretty consistent after this incident. In fighting for peace, a leader cannot enable someone to make bad choices or continue with bad attitudes. Jimmy needed to get some of his focus off himself and onto others.

In one of those first conversations, I asked him how he thought people saw him. After some time to contemplate, Jimmy began to recognize that people were avoiding him, getting frustrated with him, and even snapping at him. We discussed his good attributes and how to highlight them. Jimmy was funny and creative and on good days he made people feel important. I helped him devise a game plan that would help him use his natural attributes to put his focus on others.

Week by week, practice by practice, service by service, Jimmy got better. In fact, he was able to restore the broken relationships and become a valued member of the team. I never again heard from anyone that they did not want to play with him. Occasionally Jimmy still regressed, but even on those occasions everyone trusted he was moving in the right direction because they knew him better. When we put our focus on others rather than on ourselves, it's amazing how we gain new perspective. We will talk more about this in a later chapter.

These three well-intentioned worship leaders who worked with Jimmy were temporarily tripped up by what Paul encouraged us to do in Ephesians 4: be humble, gentle, patient, and bear with one another in love. Paul was smart, and he knew that these four things are not as easy as they sound.

For several years, *American Idol* dominated the Nielsen ratings on television. Each season this singing competition would start with tens of thousands of hopefuls. By the end of each season, through nationwide voting, America would pick a winner—the American Idol. Some seasons saw more than 30 million viewers. In three of the more popular early years, one of the judges was Kara DioGuardi, a talented songwriter, whose résumé is impeccable. Kara offered informed guidance to the singers and gave her assessment of each performer's future.

I did not like Kara. I found her arrogant, prideful, rude, demeaning, and self-indulgent. Instead of celebrating the talent on stage and giving these kids a chance to shine, she tried to make the show about herself. When I found out that after three seasons she was leaving the show, I was happy.

One day, knowing my Kara disdain, my wife, Cami, brought me a magazine article about the judge. The article was a review of a book Kara had written titled, *A Helluva High Note*. The reviewer shared how Kara had been molested repeatedly as an eleven-year-old. Years later she was date raped by a powerful producer, and after that, she was harassed sexually by another industry insider. By the end of the article, something in me had changed. I understood a bit about her. My heart actually softened.

Kara's past had caused her to put up a wall around herself that no one could enter. She was tough on people because life was tough on her. She was rude and demeaning because she had been treated terribly. A big piece of who she was had been taken away from her over and over again. Again, our struggles never give us license to act poorly toward others, but understanding someone else's struggles helps us understand their actions.

You see, the more we know someone, the more we love them. Or the more we disdain them. There is no middle ground here. But almost exclusively, the more we know about someone and what influences them, the more we understand and appreciate where they've come from and what makes them who they are.

Relationship and Mission

Most people would say being in unity is about agreeing, or at least, not fighting.

Speaking of, I once led a youth band that experienced a lot of dysfunction. One night during practice, I finally dismissed the guitar player and drummer so they could go outside and fight. We were getting nowhere and I figured it would be better for these two guys to go ahead and get it over with. (I am neither condoning this nor necessarily providing wise council. It was just our experience in that moment.)

Typically, unity is measured in our level of good feelings about one another or in our lack of arguments. But that is not all there is to unity.

Unity is the combination of relationship and mission. If we have a good relationship and we are on the same mission together, headed in the same direction, then we have unity. Relationship itself is not enough. When Jesus, Paul, and Peter spoke or wrote about unity, it was typically in the context of our relationships among fellow believers.

That is not to say that relationships with unbelievers are not important. In fact, we should work diligently to build good, deep relationships with those who are far from God. That will be in a subsequent chapter. But *biblical* unity is about relationship and mission.

I can have a great relationship with an atheist, but we are not unified. We are on very different paths. I can have a great relationship with someone who goes to church every Sunday but whose main life objective is to make a lot of money or find his next drug, but we are not unified. Unity requires a shared mission.

On the other hand, I have a shared mission with lots of people whom I do not know well, such as pastors, worship leaders of other churches, and missionaries. We have a shared direction, but no relationship. This isn't unity either. Unity requires both.

This is also a true statement in career, family life, and even politics. If there were ever two names that symbolize American politics, they are Bush and Clinton. They have divergent ideologies, leadership styles, and visions for the country. However, after the 2004 Indonesian tsunami, President George W. Bush asked former presidents Bill Clinton and George H. W. Bush to join together to raise money for a victims' relief fund. For the first time, these two former adversaries were put into a position of collaborating on a shared mission. They each cared deeply about the relief work and along the way got to know each other well. Now, after more than a decade of working together on multiple global relief efforts, these two men are close friends. There was something about the shared mission that brought them together relationally. And now, they have real unity.

Knowing One Another

Many people have asked me how to develop a culture of knowing one another and sharing a mission. No matter how far we are from biblical unity, if we will take some of the following ideas and utilize them with our teams, we will take great steps forward.

1. **Split them up**. Divide your team into groups of three and encourage them to share one thing the other two people do not already know about them. Then let them pray for one another.

I have done this exercise with my teams dozens of times and each time meaningful, relationship-building conversations have taken place. One of my bands met two nights each week from

8:00 to 11:00. Many times we started this exercise at 10:30 or later. At least half the time I had to lock the building at midnight and let people continue their conversations and prayer. They were slowly adding knowledge about one another, growing in relationships and unity. People are hungry for real connection, but we must create space. Remember, knowledge leads to love and prayer leads to intimacy.

2. **Include everyone.** Too often in my work with churches I have seen sound people and other technologists, actors, and so on not included in unity-building-type conversations. We are all on one team! There is not a tech team that is separate from a band that is separate from a drama team and so on. We are all headed in the same direction for the same purpose. So, include everyone in your times of relationship building and prayer.

3. **Share your life story.** Encourage people to share their life story in five minutes. Put them on the clock! Have others in the group share what they've learned from the story and how they now appreciate the person more. Pray for each other and thank God for their journey.

4. **Share your faith story.** Over a few weeks allow people the opportunity to share their faith journey. This is the most intimate adventure we go on and it reveals a lot about who we are. A good question to ask is, "What are two of the most significant spiritual events that have happened in your life?"

5. **Food!** Bring cookies or snacks. It is amazing how food helps form deep relationships!

6. **Get out of here.** Create activities that are outside of church and include everyone's family. Go bowling or have a cookout. Head to the park and have everyone bring their own food. Knowing one another's family is a big step in understanding who they are.

7. **Have a coffee month.** Coordinate a process where each person on the team has coffee with each of the other people on the team. It will take some major coordination, but watch the relationships and conversations deepen quickly. Make a list of questions that each person might ask during those meetings. Some good questions might include: What were some of the most fun things you did as a child?"; and "Who are some of your role models in your life?"; and "Who are you a role model for?"

Sharing Mission

Just like having a strategy to build knowledge of each other and relationships with each other on our team, we also need a strategy to make sure we are sharing a common mission. Here are some ways we can do that.

1. *Define your shared mission.* This is the first and most critical thing we must do to get laser-focused on a shared dream. Make it simple and clear. For instance, I, along with the worship leaders I lead, have a shared mission to go to God and take other people

with us. It is easy to say and remember. We can hang our hat on it and go to battle arm in arm over that. We will die on that hill.

Many people often quote the KJV version of Proverbs 29:18: "Where there is no vision, the people perish." Also true is that where there is no shared mission, the people vanish. People do not want to be part of something that has no clear objective. Plus, without a clear, shared mission, people will create their own reason for existence. This is a perfect storm for disunity. The best thing we can do to share a mission is to have a clear one. *Go to God and take others with you.* Whatever mission statement you create, say it, teach it, live it, repeat it, and write it down for easy access.

2. *Regularly discuss and measure* everything you do by your shared mission. Did we go to God? Did we take others with us? Why or why not? What can we do better?

Years ago my team and I started evaluating our services at church using a list of simple questions. We have modified the questions several times, but all of them help us understand how effective we are at going to God and taking others with us. I include those at the end of this chapter. Create space in your weekly schedule to analyze how you are doing against your mission. This will keep you focused on the right things.

3. *Go on mission together.* Over the years I have had the privilege of going on many mission trips. In various places around the US and the world I have served as a vacation Bible school director, construction supervisor, worship leader, teacher, travel coordinator, technologist, and prayer warrior. I have served with small teams of four to five people and large teams of twenty

to thirty people. Some teams have consisted of youth and some of seniors. On some missions we had a clear focus on exactly what we were going to accomplish, and other times we showed up with a vague understanding of what would be needed. In each instance, however, the same thing happened: unity.

We were together for long periods talking about life. The longer we were together, the more we opened up about our own unique stories. Pretty soon everybody understood everyone else. We were on mission together, standing arm in arm taking on the enemy, meeting needs, and letting people know about Jesus. We were laser-focused on our shared goals. This relationship building and shared mission yielded true unity. We didn't always agree on tactics or strategies, but we were unified.

One of my favorite choirs in the country is in Las Vegas at Hope Church. Together, they consistently serve the underprivileged people in their hometown. They realize that their mission is larger than just sharing music on Sundays. It is also to share Jesus with everyone. Find a place that needs help, locally or abroad, and go. You will be amazed at how unity flourishes.

Disunity Affects Excellence

When unity is not in place, it can affect the other values. One night at band practice one of the female singers, whom we'll call Linda, left at 9 p.m.—one hour after the practice started. We were only about halfway finished and I assumed she had gotten sick or received a phone call from her family. I did not think anything more of it. Linda was back on rotation three weeks later. That night, at 9 p.m., she left again. This time I took more notice. I gave her the mean eye as she left and kept going on with practice.

Three weeks later at 9 p.m., I was ready. Linda put down her microphone, packed up her purse, and started walking for the door. I quickly finished the song we were on, dismissed myself, and ran to meet her in the parking lot.

ME: Hey, just a second, let me catch my breath (*breathe, breathe*). What's going on?

LINDA: What do you mean?

ME: Well, I just noticed that for the last three rotations, you've left rehearsal before we are finished. Is everything okay?

LINDA: Yeah, it's fine. But I get up at 5:30 every morning to get ready for work and get the kids ready for school. I can give you until 9, but that's all I can give you.

I stood for a moment and processed what she just said. Several things went through my mind: *Everybody on the team gets up at 5:30 and You could at least have talked with me about that and Who do you think you are?* But then I got this adrenaline surge that I sometimes get when I'm about to say something I shouldn't. The director leader in me wanted to say something decisive, firm, and conversation ending to let her know this was a serious issue. But the servant leader in me wanted to understand what the real issue behind her story was. Somehow I softened and the conversation continued...

Me: Okay. I'll call you later this week and we'll see if there is something we can do to work through this.

Linda: Yeah, okay. Good night.

Me: Good night.

I pondered what in the world I would say to her later in the week, and, more important, what I would say to the band members who had figured out before I did that she was leaving every practice early.

Linda's issue was not her need for sleep. It was that she really did not care that much about anybody else on the team. And she really did not care about the quality of the music we were trying to learn. She cared about herself. Disunity affects excellence. Our team was not as strong as it should have been. Our singing was not as tight as it could have been if she had sacrificed two hours of sleep every twenty-one days for the betterment of the team. But she did not see it that way. She looked at her experience only through her own lenses—not through the other people's, whom I wish she had loved.

You also see this concept clearly in band members who are not prepared or tech people who show up late. Sometimes the reason for our lack of preparation is that we simply do not care that much about the people around us. Excellence is affected by disunity.

Spotting Disunity

By the time we notice a lack of unity, the seed of disunity has been growing for quite awhile. How do we spot this seed?

As leaders we constantly monitor a room for those who don't appear to be connected or engaged, or perhaps just the opposite: those who have formed their own exclusive cliques. Sometimes it's just a look or the lack of laughter. Whatever the signs might be, keep looking for them. Ask God for His eyes, His ears, and His heart to see what only He can see—those issues that lie under the surface. If something is festering and not yet fully invasive, often it can be more easily dealt with. It's like cancer in that way. Catch it early.

If you are not a team leader, you probably know what is going on sooner than the leader. You feel it. You experience it. You see the dismissive glance, the intentional silence, or the lack of joy. When you see the seeds of disunity, deal with them. Dive in. Fight for peace!

As you can see, unity is the value that holds all the others together. It is not more important than the others, but the consequences of its failure are more profound. God's Word leaves no question about the importance of unity. Now we get to live it out. Orchestrate opportunities for relationship building. Clarify the mission and build a culture around it. Above all, fight for peace. Over time every value will be raised because unity holds them together.

Is your team not getting any better? Look to unity.

Are you bored with your services and lack of creativity? Look to unity.

Is your church not growing? Look to unity.

Do you seldom experience God's presence in your times of worship together? Look to unity.

Is worship stale or evangelism close to nonexistent? Look to unity.

If we can build real, biblical unity as a core value on our teams, we can experience anointing, evangelism, worship, and blessing. And over time, the story might change to look something like this:

ALTO AMY: Hi, are you the new singer?

NEW GIRL TAYLOR: Yeah, that's me.

ALTO AMY: Great! Welcome. *(hugs neck.)* We have been praying for more people on the team. You're an answer to those prayers. Thank you for joining us.

NEW GIRL TAYLOR: You guys do such an amazing job every week. I'm just glad to be here singing with you. I love this church.

ALTO AMY: What's not to love? This band is like my extended family. I think you'll experience that too. If you have any questions tonight about anything, be sure to ask me. I'll help you in any way I can.

NEW GUY ROBERT: *(enters and walks on stage.)* Why didn't these mics stay plugged in from Sunday?

WORSHIP LEADER EDDIE: Did I forget to tell you about the big outreach last night? They had to clear the stage for it. They were giving out clothes and toys to some of the neighborhood kids and a guy from the city council spoke. It was really cool.

ALTO AMY: Yeah, it's an annual thing we all do together as a band.

DRUMMER DAVE: It was really great. A few years ago, our band started helping out. Now the tech guys and everybody else helps too. Next year you'll be joining us for it!

NEW GIRL TAYLOR: That's great! Maybe some of them will come back this week for church.

WORSHIP LEADER EDDIE: That is what we've been praying for every week at practice.

This story, or one like it, can be yours as you raise the value of unity on your team. God will be honored and you will experience anointing, evangelism, worship, and blessing as never before!

***

What About Us?

1. Which Scripture from this chapter stood out most to you? What do you think that Scripture is saying to you personally or as a team?

2. Why do you think unity matters so much to God?

3. Have one or two people from the group take three minutes and share your life story. To the listeners: What did you learn about that person through their story? In what ways does understanding them a bit more make you appreciate them in a way you hadn't before?

4. Ask one or two people to share their life's most spiritually significant moment. To the listeners: What did you learn about that person through their story? In what ways does understanding them a bit more make you appreciate them in a way you hadn't before?

5. What area(s) of disunity do you currently see on your team? What potential areas of disunity do you see? If left unchecked, what might cause disunity?

6. Where disunity lies, what do you need to do about it as a team or as the leader?

7. Considering the idea of relationship and mission, what unity-building activities do you need to build into your team immediately?

8. Are there any areas where your team struggles with unity? What can you do to correct that?

***

As promised earlier in this chapter, here are some of the worship service evaluation questions we typically utilize.

Worship Service Evaluation Questions:

1. At what point in the service, if any, did you sense the presence of the Spirit most significantly?

2. What and how did God communicate with you personally during the service this week?

3. What was the big idea of the day? How could that big idea have been better clarified?

4. Was anything said from the platform that might have confused or distracted someone who is not used to church? If so, what was it?

5. What else in the service (language, technology, people, music, etc.) might have been distracting? How could we have alleviated the distractions before they happened?

6. Did the technology effectively help communicate the big idea?

7. How did the leaders lead people toward Jesus? Or did it seem they were either performing or disregarding the crowd altogether?

CHAPTER 6
Authenticity: Keep It Real

Sherri was late that morning. We were supposed to be on stage with microphone in hand at 10:30 for a quick sound check before singing the opening song at the 11 o'clock service. Everyone was there except her. The rest of the team ran through the song, got a decent monitor mix, and sat on the front row to wait for the service to start.

As a member of this ensemble, I was seated with my team members at the end of that row when Sherri arrived. As I handed her the microphone she was to use, I took a quick glance at her.

"You look horrible!" I whispered before I thought through that phrase and how it would sound to a seventeen-year-old girl.

"Thanks a lot," she mumbled.

"I didn't mean it like that," I said, trying to recover, but she looked as if she had just woken up. We were only minutes from taking the stage when I remembered that she had attended the same party I had the night before. I knew the friends she was with and it occurred to me that she might be hung over.

"Are you hung over?"

"No, I haven't had that much time. I'm still drunk."

With her words still hanging in the air, our group, including Sherri, took the stage to open the service with a heartfelt version of "I Am Yours, Lord."

Spirit and Truth

Around midday a woman arrived at a well to get some water. A man was there who asked her for water. She was surprised that he would even talk to her, let alone ask her to give him a drink. They carried on a conversation about water rights and about thirst and about her failed relationships. Somehow this stranger knew about her five failed marriages and her live-in lover. She quickly changed the subject, but he kept uncovering her secrets. Realizing the man was a prophet, the woman asked him where people should worship: in Jerusalem or on the nearby mountain?

The man, Jesus, then uttered one of His most famous statements—a quote that we worship leaders have read a lot during services:

> Believe me, dear woman, the time is coming when it will no longer matter whether you worship the Father on this mountain or in Jerusalem. . . . But the time is coming—indeed it's here now—when true worshipers will worship the Father in spirit and in truth. The Father is looking for those who will worship him that way. For God is Spirit, so those who worship

him must worship in spirit and in truth" (John 4:21, 23–24, NLT).

What does it really mean to worship in spirit and truth? It is important to have an answer to this question because God is actively pursuing those who worship Him in this way. It's hard to imagine, but God is in red-hot pursuit of us when we worship Him in spirit and truth.

I have heard some great explanations of what "spirit" means. Some say it means to worship with gusto and energy. Some say it means we need to worship "in the spirit" as in entering some spiritual state. Some have said it refers to the fact that we must have the Holy Spirit in us to truly worship. You can add your thoughts here. But when it comes to truth, few of us disagree on what that means. It means to be truthful. It means that we mean it. It means that we believe and live out (or sing) what we say we believe. This is worshiping in truth.

So regarding Sherri, most people would agree that she was not worshiping in truth. When she sang the lyric, "I am yours, Lord," she was not being truthful to God. She was being inauthentic. She was being truthful to me, but not to the One to whom she was singing. She was like pleather.

I am going to date myself here. When I was a kid, we had a long station wagon, which also had a seat that faced backward toward the people driving in the car behind us. My sister and I would wave until those people waved back, and then we would make faces and keep bugging them until they finally passed us. A lot of people passed us in those days. The material on those seats wasn't cloth. Not for my family. We would never have crummy cloth seats that stained and ripped, but we didn't have leather either. Leather was too expensive and haughty for us. Nope. We had some sort of man-made, leather substitute, which I call pleather.

For a while the covering was great! It was a little hard, but comfy enough and it cleaned up easily. But the distinguishing characteristic of this material is that after a few years of baking in the hot Texas sun, it would form cracks. It always seemed to crack exactly on the place where your legs would hit. Sitting down was not the problem. As you put your weight on the seat, the cracks would expand to make room for your skin. But when it was time to get out of the car, the cracks would close back up and keep a piece of your leg as a souvenir. This pinch always initiated an angry yell and a decree of hatred for the blasted seat. There were two common solutions to this problem, both of which we tried: (1) you could get a cloth seat cover (this was for the rich families); or (2) you could just put a piece of duct tape over the crack. Duct tape is awesome, by the way.

The thing about real leather is that it is the same all the way through. When you cut it and look under the surface, it is leather. From top to bottom, inside out, no matter what you do to it, it is still leather. Pleather, on the other hand, is made to look nice on the outside, but when you cut below it, you find some foreign material that is not what you thought it should be.

Another tidbit about leather and pleather is that they both look nice. But pleather is a little too perfect. Real leather, on the other hand, has character. Since it came off a real animal, it has varied colors, tones, and patterns. The imperfections are beautiful. Also, leather is built to last. Over time the top layer eventually fades and wears away, but underneath exists more leather that is just as strong as its surface. Pleather lasts awhile too, but when it starts to fade and split, the whole thing falls apart quickly. There is nothing underneath that has the strength to hold it together.

This is part of the reason God wants us to be authentic. Life is not always perfect. We go through rough patches; people sit on us over and over again—hopefully not literally. The only way we will last as worshipers committed to Christ is if we strive to be truly authentic. He is not a demanding God who wants all our time and attention because He is needy. He wants what is best for us. He wants us to thrive. He wants us to be strong all the way to the end of our lives. And He knows this will require authenticity. He does not want us to be fake and weak. He wants us to be real and strong. The Father actively pursues those who figure out how to worship this way.

Don't Sing

What should Sherri have done? Stayed home? Stayed seated on the front row when the rest of us got on stage? Showed up late so she could miss having to sing? Repented at the altar while the rest of us sang that song? Or should she have just gone along and sung exactly as she did?

What was God thinking when Sherri got up to sing that morning? In a previous chapter we mentioned that in Isaiah 1:13–15, God says, "Your incense is detestable to me. . . . I cannot bear your worthless assemblies. They have become a burden to me. . . . When you spread out your hands in prayer, I hide my eyes from you" (NIV). It is clear that from God's perspective, He would rather us not meet than simply to go through the motions. It actually burdens Him when we worship in a manner that is not true. And as we saw in Amos 5:23, God repeats this idea: "Away with your noisy hymns of praise! I will not listen to the sound of your harps" (NLT). Just because we sing songs that have God-centered lyrics does not mean that God is listening to us sing them. That is a pretty arrogant idea: that God will stop everything He is doing on a Sunday morning to pay attention to people who are not fully engaged and honest with Him.

The problem with the nation of Israel's worship was that it was just a routine. They were going through the motions. They were attending the services because it was Sabbath. There was no real life change. No passion. No yielded brokenness. It was a show. They showed up, sang two songs, had a greeting, sang two songs, had a message, and went home. They were not communing with God. They were just checking a box. They might have even started to dread Sabbath. Perhaps they longed for Sabbath afternoons when they could put up their feet and celebrate that Sabbath morning was over. In any case, their hearts were not congruent with their actions. They were not authentic in their worship.

Remember God was speaking through Isaiah to all the people of Israel. This was not just a message to the leaders, the singers, or the top warriors. Today this is not a message to only point worship leaders. Our tendency is to think through this as it relates to ourselves: *I love God for real and so this does not apply to me.* But how about the people we lead on a weekly basis? Do we have people showing up and going through the motions? Are there those who might not be living out what they say they believe?

This conversation can be uncomfortable for us. Why? For one, we don't want to judge others and their relationship with God. Also, if we are really honest, we ourselves do not always come to a worship gathering with the right frame of mind. We sometimes sing without really focusing on the meaning of the words. We come with evil thoughts, grudges, bitterness, doubt, or calculated plans to sin. What should we do about that?

Our options seem to be pretty limited:

1. Sing.
2. Don't sing.
3. Get right with God and then sing.

If Isaiah heard correctly from God, then he was right to warn us that God does not want our half-hearted worship. We must not go to Him and just sing words, which is worse than not going at all. It grieves God.

Option two is not to sing. If we are in an unrepentant mood, this is probably our best option and maybe the one Sherri ought to have taken.

The third option is always available. Confess our sins to the Lord, who "is faithful and just and will forgive us our sins and purify us from all unrighteousness" (1 John 1:9, NIV). God's mercies are new every morning (see Lamentations 3:23). There is not an instance you could go to God with a true repentant heart and be turned away. His arms are always open and He offers you grace every day. This is the option I think most pleases God. Just be honest. Go to Him in truth. Confess your sin and turn away from it. Deal properly with broken relationships. And then sing! By the way, this act of confession and repentance *is* worship.

Authenticity on Our Team

I have often wondered what might have happened if Sherri had gathered the whole team before the service, including the leader, my dad, and told us what was going on. That conversation might have gone one of many ways, but I am relatively sure she would not have been singing that day. She may have never sung again.

But don't we want that kind of environment on our teams? Don't we want a place where people can be real and honest and authentic? We do, but to what extent?

What we really want is for people to share their hurts and joys, but too often our people would rather offer safe prayer needs that don't include too much public sin. They may share about their struggle with their boss and the bitterness they are experiencing, but they won't tell us about the girl at work they are attracted to. They'll tell us about their desire to work on gluttony, but refrain from letting us know that they struggle with substance abuse or pornography or other addictive behaviors.

If they were to share those deeper, messier things with us, what would we probably do with that information? For one thing, we usually do not know what to say or where to send a person for help, so we keep silent, or worse, we judge. More immediately, we do not know whether or not that person should sing or play this Sunday.

We just stumbled on a really difficult conversation. We want people to be real and yet we must have some rules in place. There is a fine line between allowing or even endorsing sinful behavior and creating a safe place to admit failures, struggles, and regret. This has come to head several times in my leadership.

One time a lady on our team was actively involved in an inappropriate relationship with a man who was not her husband. In another instance, a male singer was saying inappropriate things to women on our team. We had a singer who used foul language on Facebook, a choir member rumored to be a drug addict, and a sound guy who quit his marriage and moved into a motel. None of these leaders came to the team and shared their weaknesses with anyone.

Why not?

For one, they were embarrassed. For another, they did not want to be kicked off the team. You see, in each of these instances, we were the best form of community they had—we could have helped them and held them accountable, but instead they chose to deal with that sin by themselves.

Every ministry leader must find their own way when dealing with tough issues within a group. Plenty of churches draw red lines on immorality and how that immorality affects individual participation. This rigid style is good for clarity and spelling out the rules, but it also creates a boundary from real authenticity. You can talk about some struggles, but let's not talk about all of them (wink, wink). Still other leaders don't want to deal with any hard issue, so they turn their backs and choose to ignore the awkward sin issue altogether, hoping it will eventually just go away. Neither of these facilitates authenticity as a team while honoring God with a holy life.

In reality, every situation is different. Every person's story has twists and turns that have brought them to the place where they are now. There is always a backstory. There is always hurt. There is always disappointment. There is always fear of the future. Every person in sin has a path that includes pain. Our objective as authentic ministry partners is not simply to assume we can cut sin out of someone's life, but rather help them get to the root of it and help them walk through a healing process. Usually they want help. Let's help them!

Clearly, there are instances when people are unrepentant and do not really want to stop whatever they are doing. These people have disqualified themselves for a season from ministry leadership. But those who want help and receive help have an opportunity to get better. Might they need to sit out of ministry leadership for a while? Maybe. For his or her own good that might be best. Is it to punish them? No way. Is it because we love them and are committed to walking through their healing together? Absolutely!

In an environment where everyone knows that everyone else is completely *for* them and wants only the best for them, true authenticity as a team can flourish. Build this into your team. Make it okay to share real issues about real life. What we all want is to be beautiful pieces of leather, imperfect and flawed, but real all the way through. It is the only way to really last.

Getting Burned

I know that you might be reading this with skepticism because you have been hurt before over a situation where you were marginalized because of your sin or struggle. Years ago I met a worship leader named Josh who was in transition between churches. I invited him to sing and play through Worship Catalyst's ministry, and soon he was leading worship in various new churches including ours. Among our team members at practice and in services, Josh was happy-go-lucky and mostly positive. He made jokes of most conversations and made everyone feel comfortable. He was great at that.

One day over lunch I was talking with Josh about his church experiences. In a moment of candor, he began to tell a story that was still so fresh that he began to weep. He had given his time, energy, and heart to a pastor who drew him in and then turned on him. Josh had jumped into leadership quickly and opened up about his pain and struggles, even his sin. The pastor ultimately used this authenticity against him, and Josh made a decision not to be open and authentic again. It was too painful.

I hear this story repeated over and over among teams, especially in the church where morality is so important and we are often judged by it. If you are among those who are too scared to share your real life because it has not turned out well in the past, I first want to say that I am sorry. You deserve to have a team who will look on you with truth and grace, as Jesus would. I encourage you to find someone with whom you can be authentic. It is amazing what one good, honest friend can do for your soul. And then, slowly but surely, start to be authentic with your team. Start small; share a frustration you have at work or a dilemma you are facing at home. As people pray for you and encourage you, build up to more challenging parts of your life until you feel comfortable being real.

Building Your Authentic Culture

So how do we start building authenticity into our team's culture? And how do we know if it is working? Answering the second question first, if people are sharing their lives—the good, the bad, and the ugly—authenticity is probably starting to take root in your team's DNA.

Getting there can be a challenge. Many churches and teams have a backstory where trust was broken when someone tried to be real. A hard line was drawn. A person was kicked off the team. A relationship was severed. If this is your team's story, acknowledge it and affirm a new way forward where people can be real. Raise the value of authenticity by sharing Scripture about it (1 John 1:8–10 is a good place to start), celebrating it when you see it, and letting people know that your team is a safe place to struggle.

Another important aspect to creating authentic culture is to be authentic yourself. It does not have to be the leader of the team who makes the difference. I had just built a new band that played for a midweek service. When we had our practices on Sunday nights, I always ended with an opportunity for people to share their prayer needs. Week after week people would either share nothing or some story about a distant relative or coworker who knew someone who had a brother-in-law whose sister had a stroke—or maybe it was a heart attack.

Eventually we added Ken, a new drummer, to the team. After Ken's first practice with us, we asked him to share a bit about himself and asked how we could pray specifically for him. He thought about it for a moment and then shared how he and his wife were really struggling because it was looking more and more like they weren't going to be able to have kids on their own. That moment of authentic hurt changed everything almost immediately. Another team member talked about their job and how they were unsure about their future. Another mentioned they had some fear developing over a medical issue that had come up. That night we had one of the most meaningful times of sharing and prayer I had ever experienced. From that moment forward, from week to week, everyone talked about real things, asking for prayer and seeking advice. All it took was one person willing to be real and genuine. Be that person!

If you are the team leader, as I have been in most situations through the years, there is a tension here. How much do we share personally? How many of our weaknesses can we let out before people start to question our leadership? Aren't ministry leaders supposed to be pretty close to perfect? Well . . . first of all, we are not! Second, there is a limit to what we can share in a group. It is probably not the best idea to tell the whole team if you think you might have an unhealthy addiction or you have a crush on someone who is not your husband or wife. But we'd better have someone with whom we can talk about these things. Secrets that are not let out will destroy us. Be completely authentic with someone and be as authentic as you possibly can with your team. It is not OK for the team to all know each other very well, but not know their leader at all.

Finally, in building an authentic culture, we must be careful not to punish people who aim at becoming more authentic. This is tricky, as stated before, but the leader must decide that a repentant sinner is welcome, and that it's okay to struggle. Young leaders often want to draw up a document of behaviors and have everyone sign it. I have seen some of these, and they include things like, "A team member must not drink," "a team member will be on time for practice every week," and "a team member must stay away from all sinful behaviors." What they mean, of course, is don't have an affair or watch porn.

It is not bad to have a clear understanding of expectations. In Acts 15 the apostles decided to have a small set of ethical guidelines for new Christians. But I would encourage leaders to look at each situation carefully and with much grace. As we discussed in the chapter on unity, we often make snap judgments about people without understanding the backstory. When we do, we risk the possibility of alienating and marginalizing people whose only real community is the one you share with them.

If you are not a leader, be authentic, and humbly accept the potential consequences of being authentic. I mentioned earlier that many years ago a team member of mine was struggling with an inappropriate relationship outside of marriage. I spent much time counseling the husband, searching for what was really going on, so I could react to the true story, and asking Jesus what in the world I should do. After a few weeks, I finally decided it was time to confront and discuss the situation with this woman who was struggling. I carefully asked questions about how she was feeling, where she was along her journey, and how it was affecting her heart. I was legitimately trying to help her find a better way, so it was important for me to understand her before asking her to understand me. I was asking careful questions and she was providing honest answers. She was hurting. She was confused. She was stuck. And she didn't like who she was becoming. But at that point she was also not fully willing to fix the situation and start working toward reconciliation.

I was sad. And I was angry because the enemy was destroying a friend—and he was pretty far along on that journey. He was having his way with her, turning her against her family in favor of a lie. He was confusing her and ruining her life. Sadly, she was in no position to lead worship. There was no sense of punishment in this conversation; we were not talking about this because I was the morality police in her life. I wanted her to win, to defeat the enemy, to find healing. I knew that God had a better way forward for her and I desperately wanted her to find it.

After an hour or so of honest dialogue, I asked her what she thought would be best as it related to her leading worship. With an immense degree of humility, somehow she managed to give a great answer: "It would probably be best for me and the team if I wasn't leading right now."

In that moment of humility God began to heal her. The next few weeks were not perfect, and at times it looked as if we would lose her forever. But in the end, she found her way back to God and her family. Eventually she started leading worship again, but with more focus and anointing. God was really in control of her life. She was yielded and obedient.

If you struggle with sin, or whatever is keeping you from fully and obediently following God and strengthening your team, be authentic like this woman was and accept some potential short-term consequences until your heart is back in it.

It is beautiful what authenticity can do. When we are real with Jesus and each other, and that value is held high, He will listen to our worship and respond to us with grace.

***

What About Us?

1. How have you experienced authenticity on your team?

2. To what degree is the culture of your team one that accepts honesty and openness, even in times of struggle and doubt?

3. Do you personally feel that you could share any weakness or struggle with your team members? Why or why not?

4. What will you do the next time you are just going through the motions and not fully engaged in the lyrics of a song?

5. What real thing about yourself that you have been unwilling to talk about would you commit to sharing with your team?

CHAPTER 7
Humility: It's Not About Me

It seems that church bands are an incubator of pride. Remember the exchange between Alto Amy and New Girl Taylor?

ALTO AMY: Hi, are you the new singer?

NEW GIRL TAYLOR: Yeah, that's me.

ALTO AMY: Great, welcome. You're not here to take *my spot* are you? (*laughs*)

NEW GIRL TAYLOR: No, no, of course not! You guys do such an amazing job every week. I'm just excited to be here with everybody. I love this church.

ALTO AMY: How long have you been coming?

NEW GIRL TAYLOR: About two months.

ALTO AMY: Wow, not long at all. I'm sure this will be a good experience for you—especially still being on your honeymoon and all.

NEW GIRL TAYLOR: What?

ALTO AMY: What?

NEW GIRL TAYLOR: You said something about my honeymoon. What do you mean?

ALTO AMY: Oh, nothing. It's just great to see the newbies like you in love with the church and the band and all.

NEW GIRL TAYLOR: You're not?

ALTO AMY: Not what?

NEW GIRL TAYLOR: In love with the band and church and all.

ALTO AMY: Oh sure. I've been here since I was twelve. In fact, I was the last person to be baptized in the old horse trough before we built this building. It's a great place as long as you know your way around the people.

Did you notice the prideful comments from Amy? First, she hints that the singers on the praise team have a competition going—"You're not here to take my spot are you?" She is letting Taylor know from the beginning that there are winners and losers, and she has no intention of being a loser. After this, Amy resorts to condescension by referring to Taylor's honeymoon and calling her a newbie. After years of being on the team, Amy finds herself in a vulnerable, insecure position and her unbridled pride fights back.

This scenario is interesting. And sad. All it takes is a singer not getting a solo, a guitar player realizing that a better guitar player just showed up, an actor missing a line, or a sound engineer having someone tell him the drums are too loud. In each of these moments, and a million more like them, something from deep within the artist starts to work its way to the surface. One minute they have a focused love for the art and the God who gave it, and the next they feel defensive, angry, hurt, or even discouraged. The root is the same: pride.

James 4:6 says that God opposes the proud and favors the humble. That is straightforward. No wiggle room there. It is as if James is asking us a simple question: "Hey, guys, you have a choice here. No biggie to me. You can choose whichever you want. Just pick one and we'll go from there. Ready? Okay, you can either have God *against* you or you can have God *for* you. Let me say it another way: you can either have God on *your* side or on the *other* side. He can either *oppose* you or *favor* you. Like I said, it's your choice. Which will it be?"

I love moments in Scripture like this that offer a fork in the road and force us to take a path. Another example is in Malachi 3:10 where the prophet says on behalf of God that we can either tithe and live *with* the blessing of God or not tithe and live *without* the blessing of God. It seems like such an easy choice. Of course I want God's blessing and of course I want God to favor me, but it is never quite that easy, is it? We have the best of intentions to respond well in every situation, but too often we succumb to pride.

A Daily Routine

Answer these questions:

1. Do you closely critique the work of other people in your field, matching yourself against them?

2. When someone gains accolades, do you become frustrated and secretly wish you would have some praise also?

3. When someone else receives credit for something you secretly did or already know, do you want to let everyone know that you are the one who did it?

4. Have you ever tried to stand out in a crowd (by the way you act, sing, play, talk, or dress) because you wanted people to know how good you are at something? Do you use big words and try to sound smart? Or put others down when they do something wrong?

If you are honest, you answered yes to some or all of these questions. It means you have pride. That might sound harsh, but these questions are a good barometer of humility. Take a minute and read them again. To which one do you answer yes most often?

Pride is something we all deal with—except, of course, for me, since I have the humility thing down pat.

Since we all still have moments of weakness, I suggest we make those questions part of our daily routine. They will help us notice pride faster.

Recently I was in a meeting with some people from my church. We were discussing ways to raise the bar on missions and discipleship. I was on a team working specifically on discipleship pathways for the church and we were supposed to give our report that night. One well-intentioned person from my team started talking about discipleship with great degrees of mastery and eloquence. It was as if he were the discipleship world authority. He had books picked out, processes to follow, scriptural backgrounds, and everything else we needed for a great discipleship process.

Had I entered the room that night with a heart of humility, the evening could have ended with everyone saying amen and we could have moved on to integration. However, all I kept thinking was, *I know this stuff. I teach this stuff. I DO this stuff every day. Who are you to tell everybody the things I already know?* Something else went through my mind at exactly the same moment: Question #3: *When someone else gets credit for something you secretly did or already know, do you want to let everyone know that you are the one who did it?*

Immediately, I asked God to give me a spirit of humility and to help me keep my mouth shut. Over the next five or so minutes, the Spirit really tempered my thoughts and I offered a few tweaks to my teammate's good plan. Honestly, even the tweaks I offered came from a place of pride. But if it were not for those humility questions becoming part of my daily routine, I would have spoken up at an inopportune time and said things I would have regretted—plus it could have made me look foolish; people can usually tell when pride has taken over a conversation.

The more we ask these questions of ourselves, the quicker we notice pride when it pops up. The next day I confessed my pride to my team member.

A Dirt Road

Pride happens when we focus on self. Humility happens when we focus on others.

Several years ago after I left a good-sized church to start Worship Catalyst and help new churches as they were forming, I also left a really cool "worship concert" series in which I was participating. Several songs I'd written were recorded on an album and a group of us were on tour singing and selling them. (I don't say this to prop myself up but to emphasize how I was feeling.) While using Craigslist to find musicians for new churches, I met a man named Mario who said he played bass and keyboard. We exchanged emails and then had a quick phone conversation about his experience and what I was looking for. I decided the best thing to do would be to head to his house and play some music with him to build a relationship and assess his ability.

Mario did not live on a paved road. And to call the road he lived on a dirt road is to insult dirt roads. His address was not even on Google Maps. That should have warned me.

Mario gave me some rough directions, which included, "Turn by the bank of mailboxes" and "there is a small white stake in the ground with a red ribbon on it."

I left my house eager to meet this guy and see if he could play. After a few minutes on the paved road, I saw the mailboxes and took a right-handed turn onto the first dirt road. Nothing against dirt roads in general, but this one was one of those washboard roads that shake the teeth out of your head and every rivet from your car. There were also potholes the size of small swimming pools scattered over the road. After dodging the holes and rattling my teeth for almost ten minutes, I finally got to the bottom of a dry ravine. Apparently it had rained recently because the road was almost completely washed out. I only had two-wheel drive, so I gingerly made my way past the ravine and kept going, feverishly looking for a white stake in the ground with a red ribbon on it before it got too dark to see. The only lights in this rural area were the light of the moon and the eyes of coyotes waiting to eat lost travelers.

I sped up because when I'm lost, I would rather get lost faster. Now I was hitting some of the large potholes and feeling my car tear apart bump by bump. Ten more minutes went by and there was not a white stake anywhere. Feeling frustrated and like a failure, I finally conceded to calling Mario and asking for more directions.

I pulled out my cell phone. No signal. I was twenty minutes down a dark dirt road in the middle of nowhere, with no cell coverage, a misaligned front end, and a temper that was starting to boil.

Maybe I'll just go home, I thought. Alone in my car I said out loud, "What am I doing here? Two weeks ago I was singing in front of a big crowd who were paying to see us. Now I'm driving down a stupid dirt road to go see a guy who doesn't care one bit if I show up. What has happened to me?"

Several moments went by. I sat quietly, giving the coyotes something to see.

I had given in to pride. Pure and simple. There was no other explanation. I needed to think through how I was feeling, but that was not the time. I prayed a simple prayer of confession, turned the car around, went back to the mailboxes, and started over. This time I found the white stake with the red ribbon on it, turned right, and started a three-year relationship with Mario, who, over time, anchored a new church band and gave his life to Jesus.

I had to deal with some hidden pride I didn't know existed. My pride wanted me to go home. Had I done that, I would have missed out on a great relationship and a profound work of God.

Paul kicks the Philippians and me in the teeth in chapter 2 when he writes,

* Don't be selfish.
* Don't try to impress others.
* Be humble.
* Think of others as better than yourselves.
* Don't look out for your own interests, but take an interest in others too.

Wait, Paul! One thing at a time here! Quit piling it on!

And then, out of the blue, Paul drops the gauntlet: "You must have the same attitude that Christ Jesus had. Though he was God, he did not think of equality with God as something to cling to. Instead, he gave up his divine privileges; he took the humble position of a slave and was born as a human being. When he appeared in human form, he humbled himself in obedience to God and died a criminal's death on a cross" (vv. 5–8, NLT).

Do you get it?

Jesus, who is God, gave up the divine privileges of being God.
I got frustrated when I had to give up paved roads.

Jesus, who is God, took up the humble position of a slave.
I wrestled with serving someone who might not care who I am.

Jesus, who is God, chose to die a criminal's death on a cross for me.
I got irritated when I had to sacrifice my car and my ego for Him.

By my actions and heart, I was saying, *It's all about me.*
By His actions and heart, He was saying, *It's not about Me.*

But it *was* about Him! And that is exactly the point. Jesus, who is God, went to great lengths to make it not about Himself. We typically go to great lengths to prove to everyone that it is about us.

It's Not about Me

Say out loud, "It's not about me."

Go ahead, say it.

"It's not about me!"

Louder!

"It's not about me!"

No matter where you are—an office, your living room, even the public library. One, two, three: "IT'S NOT ABOUT ME!"

I'm glad to hear you say that.

"I didn't get to sing lead on that song." Well, good thing it's not about you.

"That actor is getting more stage time than me." That's okay. It's not about you anyway.

"I don't like that new song." Thank goodness it's not about you then.

"We are introducing too many new people onto our team." Well, it's a good thing it's not about you.

It's not about you or me or any of us. It never has been. It never will be. It's not about your feelings or your family or your time or your schedule. It's not about your money or your ability or your sacrificial gift to God. Everything we do is only and always about Jesus, the Lamb of God who sacrificed His life for our sin. Period. Peace out.

Here is an idea: wake up every morning, look in the mirror, and say to yourself, "It's not about you." Then go and face people and situations with perspective. Have grace with people, as Jesus did. Forgive people, as Jesus did. Make yourself lowly and raise others up, as Jesus did. We have a great and beautiful model for humility: it is Jesus.

Prima Donnas and Self-Conscious Pride

Have you ever met a prima donna? They are huge amounts of fun. They expect people to serve and honor them. When they perform they expect a certain response. A while back, Beyonce's venue demands were made public. The green room had to be exactly 72 degrees; she would eat only on clean, white tablecloths with linen napkins. She required two white area rugs and a blender, among other things. Amazingly, Beyonce's requests are mild compared to some other divas. Many of their requirements make sense (water bottles, food, private restrooms, etc.). But somewhere along the way, some people start to see themselves as more important than the people around them.

The pride that oozes off a prima-donna-type person is easy to see: they believe in themselves and truly see themselves as better than most people at whatever they do. In their minds they have measured everyone and found themselves to be among the best. Have you ever known someone like that? This attitude can be really damaging in a church.

I'm sure you are thankful that you are not like that. You are not prideful. In fact, you are shy and self-conscious. You would rather hide than be the center of attention. There are things about yourself you simply do not like. This comes off as humility, but it is pride. Self-consciousness is self-centeredness and self-centeredness is pride. Sorry to be the bearer of that bad news. The enemy is on the attack and wants to destroy the self-conscious person by putting more and more of their attention on themselves.

How do we work through this? First of all, we must admit to the pride we have in our hearts—whether it is self-confident pride or self-conscious pride. Next, we need to confess it to Jesus, repent, and move on to the final step, which is . . .

Serve Others

Paul told the Philippians to consider others better than themselves. The most direct and easy way to do this is to serve others. Help them set up their equipment. Offer to watch their children during a practice. Give the lead parts to someone else. Work in a homeless shelter. Sacrificially give someone money without them knowing who gave it. Volunteer your time to help someone move. Do something. Serve someone. Consider others as better than yourself. As we serve others we will push back pride and usher in humility personally and as a team. It really is that simple.

Reinforcing Humility

Our teams must be humble. Humility is a value, a boundary we cannot cross, or we will not reach our goal of going to God and taking other people with us. Here are some ways to reinforce humility on your team.

1. *Talk about it.* Build a culture in which it is normal to confess pride to one another. Confessing pride demonstrates humility.

2. *Teach it.* Find places in the Bible that deal with humility and pride and discuss them as a team. For instance, Proverbs 27:2, Mark 9:35, Luke 14:7–11, and Philippians 2:1-11.

3. *Pray for every person on your team* every day for a month. Prayer softens our hearts for people.

4. *Call it out.* If you are a team leader, it might be necessary at times to humbly confront someone about the pride they have.

You are serving them by calling it out, because the pride will destroy them eventually and it is already bringing harm to the team. Before calling it out, however, it is important to find the root of the pride. Sometimes it is deep hurt or mistrust, fear or disappointment. Remember that pride is not from God, so something unhealthy has developed it in us.

5. *Be humble.* A humble, godly life is beautiful and attractive. People will be drawn to it and will want to model it themselves. Even if no one around you is humble, be humble anyway. Let them have their way. You will be better off for it—and so will they.

The Enemy and Pride

You see, our "enemy, the devil, prowls around like a roaring lion looking for someone to devour" (1 Peter 5:8). That someone is you . . . and me. He knows how to get to you. He knows your weaknesses and frailties, your insecurities and your deepest desires. The enemy knows that a fast track to your destruction is pride. He also knows that the fastest way to derail a team is through pride.

Satan would love for us to get our attention off God and on to ourselves. He does not really care if we focus on him (become worshipers of the devil), he just wants us not to focus on God. That is a real worship killer. That is a win for him.

The arts as a whole are very individualistic. We sing, play, act, do technology, etc. Even though we often perform in a team, the act of producing the art is still singular. It is easy to get wrapped up in ourselves when this is the case. *Did I perform well? Did people enjoy my singing? Am I better than the next guy or girl?*

How people respond to us has a lot to do with how we feel about ourselves. Do not get caught in that trap. You are a child of God, created in His image to do amazing things in His Kingdom. That is your identity. You are not primarily a singer or actor or technologist. You are God's son or daughter. Period. That is who you are. As His child, He has given you certain abilities that are to be used for Him as He sees fit. They are given by Him, for Him.

The enemy wants you to see yourself as a singer or player or dancer, but God says you are more than that: you are His. That is way better, and it gives us perspective.

It keeps us humble.

***

What About Us?

1. Which of the four questions at the beginning of the chapter do you answer yes to most often?

2. What are some ways that you have seen pride show up in teams you have been part of in the past?

3. Would you consider yourself a confident person or a self-conscious person? How has that led you toward pride?

4. What step(s) are you going to take to combat your pride?

5. What are some ways you can serve others—considering them better than yourself?

CHAPTER 8
Evangelism: Lost People Matter to God

Every day 153,000 people die.[1] That is 6,375 souls each hour and 106 every minute. In fact, in the length of time it will take you to read this sentence, another 10 people will have entered into an eternity somewhere. The harsh reality is that the vast majority of these people will enter into an eternity without Christ.

How does that make you feel? Any grief? Any sadness? Any sense of desperation?

This is probably not the way you would have wanted to start a chapter. But if we are going to discuss honestly the values we share on our teams, we must talk about this value: Evangelism. In other words, lost people matter to God. And since they matter to God, they should matter to us. If we get outside the boundary of this value, we will never get to our goal of going to God and taking others with us. You see, if we choose to put our focus on ourselves, our teams, and other believers, living our lives away from the community of nonbelievers, we will live outside of God's plan for us.

A Rude Awakening

A number of years ago, from the padded seats on the second row of my church, I had a rude awakening. The band and I had just finished singing a few praise songs and we were feeling good about ourselves. We were making some strong progress together. People were constantly talking about how we were sounding great, and they even believed a movement of God was starting. The church was also growing fast, and the long hours we were putting in were starting to pay off. I crossed my arms, sat back in my chair, and settled in for another sermon, satisfied that I had done my part to help the congregation prepare for the words that were about to come their way.

And then Tony stepped up to preach. Tony wasn't our normal pastor. Not that he was completely abnormal, but in many ways, he was . . . and is. One of Tony's distinguishing characteristics is that he wakes up every morning and goes to bed every night with a true broken heart for people who are far from God. On this particular day his sermon started simply enough. He had us take a piece of white computer paper and a pen.

"Everybody, write down the names of your immediate family members who are not Christians," he said. No big deal here; I grew up in a Christian home and I was married to a great Christian woman.

"Next, write down some distant family members whom you sometimes see who don't know Jesus." Well, like I said, both

Cami and I grew up in Christian homes and both sides of my family have a rich Christian heritage.

"Next, write down the names of your coworkers who are far from God." Okay, I worked at the church where I was sitting. I sometimes wondered if a few of my fellow staff members were Christians, but I had to assume they were all followers of Jesus.

My piece of paper looked very white and empty.

"Almost done," Tony said. "Now write down the names of people on your street and around your neighborhood who don't know Jesus." I had just moved to a new neighborhood and did not know one person on my street. As the piece of paper stayed blank, I started to feel very convicted. I wanted desperately to write down someone's name, but I realized that I did not have one lost person in my life.

"Finally, write down the names of any acquaintances you have who do not have a relationship with Jesus. Maybe you know people from the coffee shop or the grocery store. Maybe there is someone on the bus with whom you occasionally have a conversation. What about the attendant at the gas station you frequent or your waiter at your favorite restaurant? This is really anyone around you with whom you have any degree of relationship whatsoever. Write down their names and then hold up the sheet to show it to me."

People around the room held up pieces of paper filled with names of souls who needed a relationship with Christ. Tony looked around the room at the sheets and made a few comments about how the area around our church had so many people who were far from God. I sat staring at my blank, white, lineless paper. I felt like everybody in the room was looking at me. But I also felt completely alone, ready for a reprimand from a pastor, myself, or maybe even God.

The rest of the message was focused on specific ways to build the kinds of relationships with these people that could potentially lead them to beginning a life of faith. All I heard was, *Blah, blah, blah,* you loser!

Somehow I had so immersed myself in church and Christian culture that I had forgotten the clear calling I had from God. Ironically, one of the reasons I was at that church in the first place was because of its evangelistic fervor. The lead pastor was the pacesetter in this passion. One year earlier I'd sat in his office trying to determine whether or not I would take this worship pastor job. He shared with me his heart for the lost in the community. And in his office, just sitting there talking about nameless people, he began to weep. My only thought was that I wanted to be in an environment like this—where the lost were held in such high regard. So I took the job and immediately began building my Jesus bubble.

With blank sheet of paper in hand, I headed home. Something had to be done.

Cami and I talked about it and thought through the different ways we could trade in some time, focus, and energy and recalibrate it toward people who needed the light and salt we had.

The next day we joined a tennis club. In a healthier previous life I had been a pretty good tennis player and I always missed playing. This was my chance to build relationships with far-from-God people, get in shape, and do something I enjoyed. It was actually refreshing to be in a real community of cussing, drinking, broken, lost people. I relished those years of real community—traveling tournaments, Monday Night Football parties, and team competitions. Along the way, the people found out what I was all about, and through conversations about Christ, many of them took deeper steps toward faith.

That season ended and the gravitational pull toward the Jesus bubble started again. You see, it is easy and safe for Christians to hang out with Christians doing Christian things in Christian places for Christian causes, all in the name of Jesus Christ. It's not that having Christian relationships is bad, but when the vast majority of the people we know and hang out with are already followers of Jesus, we slip into an existence that the enemy loves—one where we forget who we are called to be. Yes, I am suggesting that it is our responsibility and calling to reach a dark world with the gospel, the Good News about Christ. For every problem, He is the solution. For every depression, He is the joy. For every broken relationship, He is the reconciler. For every sickness, He is the healer. For every fatherless person, He is the perfect dad. For every wounded heart, He is the comforter. For every addiction, He is the One who pulls us out. For every wandering soul, He is the direction-giver. He is all of these things and more for every person who will call on His name.

If we really believe this and love God enough to let Him influence our love for others, we will want to run up to every far-from-God person we can find and tell him or her that there is hope. But sometimes we just think of Christ as ours, as if we own Him, and we see lost people as if they are in the way of our Christian culture. Yet who will tell them if we don't?

The apostle Paul clears this up for us in Romans 10:14–17, where he says that faith comes from hearing the good news about Christ and the good news is imparted by people who are sent. That is you and me. You are sent. We are sent. We have been commissioned to "Go into all the world and preach the Good News to everyone" (Mark 16:15, NLT). We don't have to wait around for another calling or something more specific. We have it! We never have to ask God if He really wants us to tell someone about Jesus. That answer was cleared up two thousand years ago. The answer is yes!

Remember this is a value, a barrier we cannot cross. Why? It comes down to obedience. After reading Mark 16:15, we see that we have this charge to share the Good News of Jesus with others. If we refuse to do that or do not make it a priority, we are not being obedient to this charge. This makes us inauthentic. We would be singing, "Take my life, Lord—except I don't want to talk about Jesus to people who don't know You." We become my drunk singing friend from two chapters ago, singing the songs, but with a heart not yielded to Him. This is why we must keep this on the list of values.

A Link in a Chain

In that season of tennis playing evangelism, I developed a friendship with a guy who was originally from India. Between games, in the middle of a great match between us, I started asking about his Hindu heritage. He discussed his family, their beliefs, and where he stood on the issue as an adult. I was truly interested because he was a friend. After he shared, he asked me what I thought. Immediately my heart started racing. My mouth got a little dry and I started saying some random words to buy time while I tried to remember the whole Roman Road to Salvation. I was legitimately afraid that I would mess up this moment, damaging any possibility of my friend learning about Jesus properly and giving his life to God. I do not remember much of anything I talked about, but I am sure it was not profound. There might have even been a moment when I regretted that I had brought up the whole religion conversation in the first place.

The biggest reason we do not engage in conversations about Jesus with far-from-God people is that we are afraid of what the person might ask us or think about us. We are afraid of annoying someone, offending them, or sounding "holier than thou." This is understandable. Nobody wants to be "that guy" who is always throwing around "praise Jesus" and "hallelujah" and making everybody around him or her uncomfortable. Also, nobody wants to wreck a good relationship with an awkward conversation about faith. I have been there.

We also have a fear of failure. This was my fear with my Indian friend. What if he doesn't get on his knees right then and there, confess all of his sins to God, and give his life over fully to the grace of Jesus? What if all I do is muddy things up or confuse him? What if I don't have the right answers to his questions and I do more damage than good?

Fear. Where does it come from? In 2 Timothy 1:7, the apostle Paul wrote to his disciple Timothy that fear comes from somewhere other than God. God gives us a spirit of power, love, and sound mind, not a spirit of fear. So the panic must be from the enemy who is coaxing us to keep our mouths shut and not offer words of life. It would be detrimental to his campaign of destruction if we kept boldly sharing with people that there is a better way to live.

My experience is that most people with whom I share the Good News about Jesus do not immediately pray and give their lives to Him. Most of them are appreciative and thoughtful in the conversation, but few are at the place where they are ready to respond. I am a link in the chain that is leading to their salvation. I am one of several people or groups who will influence this person toward Jesus.

The fun thing is that we never know where we are in the chain. Many times we are an early link, just awakening someone to the idea that they might need a Savior. Other times we are closer to the end where someone has been thinking about it for a while and still has questions about how it all applies to them. On occasion, God gives us the privilege of sharing with someone who is already close to making a decision. We get to help them take the step between considering faith and starting a conversation with Christ that will continue for the rest of their lives. In any of these cases, we are a link in the chain. And each link is just as important as the last one.

As links, do we have the responsibility of that person's decision? No. Do we have control over how they will respond? No. Do we need to feel horrible about our performance if they don't respond positively? No. Our job is to share. God's job is to move. Do not fear. Just share.

What to Share

Share your story. Revelation 12:11 says that they overcame by the blood of the Lamb and the word of a testimony. It is your story that will help people respond. If you do not know all the answers, it's okay—you have a firsthand account of the cleansing work of Jesus. Share that.

John 9 is a story about a man who had been born blind. Jesus healed him on the Sabbath and gave him sight. It was a big deal for Jesus to do this on the Sabbath because the Jewish law forbade someone from working on that day of the week. The Jewish leaders questioned the formerly blind man and his parents. After a lengthy exchange, the Pharisees finally asked the man about Jesus, suggesting that Jesus was a sinner. The healed man said, ""I don't know whether he is a sinner," the man replied. "But I know this: I used to be blind, but now I can see!" (v. 25 CEV)

This man was not theologically trained or ready to answer a lot of questions about faith. All he knew was his personal experience with Jesus, as short as it was. The Pharisees did not kneel down and surrender the control of their lives to Christ (though that would have been awesome). Instead they ended up throwing the healed man out of the room. There was a response. It was their personal response and was in no way improperly influenced by the healed man. He just told his story. How the Pharisees responded was up to them.

Create Opportunities

I love going to my community's grocery store deli. I love eating meat, and the deli has a lot of different kinds of meat. The guy who shaves the turkey and cheese for my family is a twenty-eight-year-old man who seems to enjoy his job. He works from 4–11 p.m. most days. He loves playing pool on Thursday nights, and he lives with his family in another part of town. He is fun to talk to when things are not too busy at the deli, which is after 8 p.m. So instead of getting two pounds of turkey and lots of cheese slices to make it through the week, I choose to get small amounts and head back every few days, usually late at night. This man knows me. He sees me coming and says hi. He knows what I order. He also knows that I pray for him and care about what is going on in his life.

At the checkout line is another young man. He is energetic and courteous and also works the late shift. I get to the grocery store several times each week to pick up a few items, so during each trip I find his line and go through it. Even when the line is long, I wait patiently for the opportunity to talk with him. He lives with some family members and is saving up money to become a freelance photographer. He will be taking my family pictures next season.

While I love going to the grocery store, heading out to the bank is a different story. In fact, I love ATM machines, direct deposit, and online banking. When taking pictures of checks became an acceptable route for depositing money, it was like Christmas. You mean I don't have to fight traffic and head to the bank anymore? This is awesome! But recently I had to go to the bank to set up a few accounts for the church we are planting. The banker who helped me is really nice and interested in what I have going on in my life. She has a son and they live with her dad. She moved to Las Vegas to help him because he is getting older.

The first time I met her I invited her to come to our church, once we started meeting. Now, each week I forgo the "inconveniences" of online deposits, ATMs, and drive-through lines for the great "convenience" of getting out of my car and walking inside to stand in line. Every time I do, she stops what she is doing; we talk about the church and carry on a short conversation.

If you are like me and you spend your life in a Jesus bubble, get out of it and find some people who are far from God with whom you can build relationships. They are not projects. They are friends. They are probably not going to seek you out, so you will have to seek them out. They are not going to go out of their way to connect with you, so you will have to go out of your way to connect with them. God places these people in our lives almost every day and often we miss it.

Here is a way to think about it: I am in the cafe at Fry's Electronics as I write this today. It was not my intention to come to Fry's, but last night I noticed that the power cable on my Mac had a short in it. So I had to suffer and head to Fry's, the largest cool-stuff store in the world. I can spend a lot of time and even more money here if I'm not careful. As we enter into places like Fry's, grocery stores, malls, or the places we work, we each have an important question to answer. *Why am I here?*

This is a natural guy question. We are hunters. If we need jeans, we walk into the store, head straight to the jeans section, pick out a pair, maybe try them on, and then walk out with our prize . . . hopefully all within five minutes. If we are going to a grocery store to get bacon, eggs, and milk, we mentally map out the path we will take before we ever get to the store so we can beat our best record. Nothing can stop us. We are on a mission. Everything else is a distraction.

But what if you thought of a simple trip to the store in this way: instead of going in with an agenda to hunt and gather, what if you stopped outside the store and prayed: "Lord, what would you have me do in the store today? If there is someone for me to influence in some way, let me see the open door and I will walk through it." When you walk through the doors of that business, you will walk in as a missionary, not as a consumer. You will still get whatever you came in for, but you will have a new mission. Many times nothing magical will happen, but sometimes God will open a door wide for you to start a conversation.

Starting Conversations

Las Vegas, my city, is a pretty unfriendly place once you get off the strip. People do not engage in conversation much. I especially see it when I hang out in the school parking lot, waiting to pick up my daughter. There are several hundred parents standing around and it is completely quiet—no one talks to each other. At home, most people have a garage so they can drive into it and hide. They believe life is best lived in seclusion. In this environment, people are not going to come up to me and start talking. It has to be me. And it has to be you. That means we have to create opportunities and start conversations. Try these questions on your waiter or convenience store clerk:

* How is your day going today? (Depending on their answer
. . .)
* What could make it better? (Or . . .)
* Awesome, what makes today such a good day?
* If they say, "I'm almost off" or "I have a long day ahead of me" ask,
* "What do you like to do with your time when you're not at work? (Or . . .)

* Do you have any big plans for the weekend?

There are hundreds of questions like this we can ask. We are not prying; we are just starting a conversation that God can use. If we keep our head down and wait for someone to engage us, we don't put ourselves in a position to be used by God. Once we get a short conversation started, we can notice if Jesus is opening a door or not. If He is, we walk through it. Offer life. Give encouragement. Promise that we will pray. Tell them Jesus loves them. Leave them with something significant. They do not have to kneel there and pray. You and I are a link in a chain.

Lost People Matter to God in Our Worship Services

When we say we have a shared goal of going to God and taking others with us, we need to decide who those "others" are. "Others" is everyone—both lost and saved. As worship leaders we must care deeply that everyone in the room is experiencing the life-changing love of Christ. We are taking Christians to Jesus, and we are taking far-from-God people to Him as well. Everyone can experience Him in some way. The question is no longer simply whom a worship service is for (seeker, believer, etc.), the question is how do we communicate to the people who are there?

With this question in mind, we can start to pay attention to our language. Do we say things that don't make sense to people who are not well versed in the Bible and church?

"Let's stand and honor the Redeemer King as we raise our voices in praise unto Him." Or would it be better to say, "One way we can say thanks to God is to sing. This song has lyrics that help us do that."

If you say the first one, some people will think, *Say what?* If you say something like the second one, using the same kind of language you would use in normal conversation, everybody will understand what you are saying. Plus, you will be more authentic. Also, please do not ask for an amen at the end of every sentence. Amen?

Song lyrics can be just as confusing. During one worship service a few years ago, we were singing a song called "At the Cross" and we got to the bridge, which says, "You tore the veil, You made a way when You said that it is done." I was looking at the expression on the faces of some people and realized we were creating confusion. We had a lot of people in the room who did not know about the veil in the temple or even the phrase, "It is finished." I could tell many folks were thinking about why someone would tear the only veil they had ever seen—a wedding one. This was a teaching moment.

I stopped the song in mid-flow and said, "Hey guys, in case you don't understand what this part of the song is referring to, let me tell you a story. During the days of Jesus and way before that, the presence of God was in a room in a temple in Jerusalem and a curtain covered that room from the rest of the world. Basically, people were separated from direct access to God by a curtain. Can you imagine what it must have been like when someone was walking by the temple the day Jesus died? Right at the moment when Jesus said his last words, "It is finished" and died, the curtain tore apart from top to bottom. At that moment, for the first time, that person realized that no longer was there any separation between God and humanity. For the first time ever, they had direct access to God. And because of what Jesus did, we also have direct access to God!"

People actually started applauding. They did not know that information. All they needed was a little help. We sang it again, and this time I thought the roof might come off the place. Think through how understandable your songs and words are, especially to people who are far from God. Amen?

Spotting This Value

This value, when it is being owned and lived out by the people on your team, is easy to spot. People will talk freely about their friends who need Jesus. They will tell each other about opportunities they have had to share their faith story with someone, or new doors they see God opening. More people who are far from God will attend the church, and you might even have one on the platform acting or playing in the band. In essence, the conversation shifts from talking about self and team to talking about others. This is a value that will feel the most Christ-centered when it is right. Your team will be on mission together.

Ingraining the idea that lost people matter to God, while easy to spot, is often difficult. The longer churches are in existence, the harder this value is to foster. The gravitational pull for any team is inward. The team must battle to stay focused on raising up this value until it's rooted in its members.

The best way to cultivate it is to live it. Build relationships with lost people and then share stories of how it's going. It is messy; it is not quick, and it is entirely contagious. When I am around someone who really cares about people who are far from

God and talks about them with passion and love, it reminds me and gets me excited about one of the reasons God made me: to tell others about Him.

One more suggestion. Make sure you always have lost people in your services. Nothing will rivet you to the mission more than having a lost person sit in your church. It heightens your awareness of the things you say and do as nothing else can.

Finally, in the time with your team, pray for one another's friends who need Jesus. Pray for them by name and then celebrate as these friends come to a place of faith, because God's love in us drives our love for lost people.

Whenever I want to remind our team of how important lost people are to God, I pull out this Scripture and read it to them. I hope it will inspire you as well.

At one time we thought of Christ merely from a human point of view. How differently we know him now! This means that anyone who belongs to Christ has become a new person. The old life is gone; a new life has begun!

And all of this is a gift from God, who brought us back to himself through Christ. And God has given us this task of reconciling people to him. For God was in Christ, reconciling the world to himself, no longer counting people's sins against them. And he gave us this wonderful message of reconciliation. So we are Christ's ambassadors; God is making his appeal through us. We speak for Christ when we plead, "Come back to God!" For God made Christ, who never sinned, to be the offering for our sin, so that we could be made right with God through Christ. (2 Corinthians 5:16–21, NLT)

***

What About Us?

1. What part of the 2 Corinthians passage above stands out to you or speaks to you the most? What do you think Jesus might be saying to you?

2. Name three people with whom you are building a relationship who do not have a personal relationship with Jesus. What are you doing to build those relationships?

3. What are some next steps in your personal evangelism?

4. Are your worship gatherings attainable for people who are far from God?

5. What are some additional ways you can use your worship gatherings to give people an opportunity to follow Christ?

CHAPTER 9
Party: More Than Just Having Fun

Bill pastored a small, new church in a suburban area outside of Tucson. He knew that one of his biggest responsibilities was to build a worship team that would engage the community with music and other art forms. After they had been meeting for a few months, Bill asked me to help him build the team. I said yes and we got started. When I arrived for the first time at their band practice in Bill's home, I was surprised to find four people on the team. I assumed it would be one . . . or none. I listened to them struggle through two songs and then completely butcher a third. It was definitely going to take some hard work to get this team sounding good.

About thirty minutes into practice I started to smell something incredible. I was giving direction to the group and some of the individuals, but my mind and stomach were starting to be distracted by what my nose was enjoying. Five more minutes went by and then I heard Bill say, "Okay guys, it's ready." I turned around and saw two large, freshly baked pizzas. They looked amazing. We all took a break from practice and enjoyed Bill's amazing cooking. Before we ate, he asked for any prayer requests and praises. The four teammates talked about their lives. Two were in high school, one was an elementary-school teacher with grown kids, and the fourth was an older man who worked for the city.

They shared their daily experiences as if they were family. They asked each other great questions and seemed to genuinely care when it was time to pray. During our pizza break, there was almost constant laughter as all four team members and the pastor shared stories and jokes. We eventually got back to practice and made good progress. It was a great place to be on a Tuesday night.

I attended those practices for more than a year as we added team members and progressed as a band. Every single time I was there, we had food. And every single time I was there, we laughed. This group had figured out something: life, and band practice, should be fun.

What Are We Really Talking About?

What does it mean to party? When I am confused about something and want to find out its real meaning, I typically go to one place to discover the intricacies of that elusive concept. It is not Webster's dictionary or the Encyclopedia Britannica. Those don't have street cred or real reliability. No, I need to find a clearinghouse that I can really trust—one that has stood the test of time and has had each definition and explanation vetted by the world's best minds.

That's right. I go to Wikipedia. Why not? It is available and consistent. I can find information on sports and news, companies and people. Wikipedia is a beautiful mixture of history and pop culture, dictionaries and encyclopedias. In fact, it even has "pedia" in it, which means knowledge. And it has "wiki" in it, which means everybody can be smart and speak about whatever they want to. So, in essence, it is a site of shared knowledge where we can all add our two cents about anything we think we might know something about. Great, huh?

So I headed to Wikipedia and looked up the word party. Almost every friend I have ever known who "parties" talks about getting drunk or high.

> "Man, we really partied last night!"
> "When I was in college I really knew how to party."
> "Party on, Wayne." "Party on, Garth."

But my assumption was that *party* has more to it than simply partaking. I was right! Here is part of the definition of *party* as designed by you and other members of the global knowledge army:

A party is a gathering of people who have been invited by a host for the purposes of socializing, conversation, recreation, or as part of a festival or other commemoration of a special occasion. A party will typically feature food and beverages, and often music and dancing or other forms of entertainment. Some parties are held in honor of a specific person, day or event, such as a birthday party, a Super Bowl party, or a St. Patrick's Day party.

Isn't that a great definition? By the way, Webster's definition is only eleven words. Take that, Mr. Webster!

Wikipedia says that some parties are held in honor of a specific person, day, or event, such as a birthday party. It seems, as adults, we require this kind of event to truly party.

Recently I went to a party at a house where thirty or so people had gathered to hang out, eat finger foods, and drink out of red plastic cups. I knew most of the people in the room and enjoyed connecting with them. We talked, laughed, and told stories. As the party wound down, I heard several people say, "We should do this more often."

What were they saying? They were articulating a feeling to which we need to listen carefully: *This is more fun than my normal life.*

For some reason they had allowed themselves to get to a daily place where they weren't having fun. This happens when someone has a crummy job, a horrible boss, a stressed home life, or financial troubles. Of course, there are hundreds of reasons someone might think a party is better than their real life, but ultimately for them to experience fun, it has to be separate in some way from their real life.

But this *value* of party is not really about an event. In fact, none of the values we have discussed so far are event-driven. You can't generate humility by having a humility event. You can't create an evangelistic ethos in your team by having a one-time evangelistic event. And you can't create a party DNA in your team by having a party. It is deeper than that. It is a daily experience. A party value is in full form when people show up and have a good time together, no matter what they are doing. When they are together, it feels like a party.

I am writing this chapter in my local public library (thank you, tax dollars). I'm in this quiet room of adults who are all on their computers doing whatever it is they do. They look busy and focused. Everyone is facing one direction, toward a big window that overlooks an area with kids' books and toys.

About five children are playing with crummy plastic toys, while one or both of their parents enjoy a few minutes of quiet reading or napping. There is not that much for the children to do. The toys are simple, the area is small, and the signs everywhere tell them to be quiet. But they are having the time of their lives! Built into a child is a party DNA. They are always ready for a good time.

We adults get too stressed about family and jobs and life, and often we stop having fun. Cami and I used to have some friends we hung out with several nights a week after work. We played games, watched movies, ate unhealthy food, and laughed a lot. Many weeknights we found ourselves crashed out in one of our family rooms not quite able to make it through the last part of the movie. The next morning we were all at work on time, smiling, and ready for whatever the day might bring. We were living "party." That value was deeply entrenched in our lives.

Maybe we can resurrect the party DNA. Maybe we can create such a party atmosphere in our teams that no matter what we are doing, it is uplifting, refreshing, and full of joy.

Before doing that, however, we need to discuss whether or not this ideal really matters. In this book I have discussed some pretty strong theological values, which we all need in our lives and on our teams: excellence, creativity, unity, humility, authenticity, and evangelism. By now we all agree they are critical for a team's development. However, some intellectuals have rolled their eyes at me when I have discussed party. So let's make sure we see what the Bible has to say about it.

Solomon and Par-tay

One step on my path from a *party hardy* mentality to being a serious and intellectual adult (or something like that) was when I read the Old Testament book of Ecclesiastes.

At age nineteen, after reading Ecclesiastes 2, I decided that nothing I would do would ever matter. The book's author, a wealthy ruler named Solomon, wrote that everything was meaningless, a chasing after the wind, that nothing under the sun was new.

He had tried everything. God had granted him more wisdom than anyone else (see 1 Kings 3), yet Solomon said it had no meaning. He did not deny himself *any* pleasure: wine, lovers, possessions, but none of it mattered. For some reason, he even took seven hundred wives and three hundred other women into his harem. (Solomon claimed that in all of this his wisdom never left him, but I choose to differ: he had *seven hundred* wives!)

He built houses and planted vineyards, established gardens and great irrigation systems. He bought slaves and had more herds and flocks than anyone around. Ultimately, he amassed more stuff and became greater than any person in the history of

Jerusalem and probably the world. Think Bill Gates on steroids. But at the end of his efforts to find purpose, nothing he created would suffice. It was all as meaningless as chasing after the wind.

Except for one thing. In verse 10, Solomon wrote that he took delight in all of his labor. The work itself, he actually enjoyed. The *act* of building homes and planting trees, growing plants and digging ditches were enjoyable to him. In fact, in 3:12–13, Solomon finally drew a conclusion to all of his work:

> I know that there is nothing better for people than to be happy and to do good while they live. That each of them may eat and drink, and find satisfaction in all their toil—this is the gift of God. (NIV)

My NIV Study Bible reference says that, essentially, Solomon is admitting that God's people find meaning when they cheerfully accept life from God's hand. It is only possible to enjoy the work when we see it in the context of God's activity in our lives.

A good friend taught me something about that. Every day he sat behind a desk at his high-stress job of designing parts for airplanes. Some days were fine and others were crummy. His bosses often threatened to fire him and tried to make him feel he was not good enough for the job. It was an output-oriented, 100-million-dollar work environment that caused many to burn out and quit. But every time I saw my friend, he wore a smile and was quick with a laugh. The environment and his bosses might have been trying to bring him down, but he would not fall.

One day I asked him, "How can you always be the same guy when these work circumstances should drag down your outlook?"

His reply: "On my desk I have a picture of my wife and my three kids. Whenever I start to feel like I might lose it, I look at them and remember why I have a job in the first place. It is to provide for them. They are a gift from God and if all I have to do is take a cheap shot every now and then, that's not a problem. My family is worth that."

My friend's perspective is that of Solomon's. The thing he was building was not as important as the building process itself. We often get caught up in the events surrounding our activity, whether it be for pay or not, and we forget to enjoy the moment we are in right now. That moment is a gift from God.

Solomon had a good time working. It was when he stopped and started to ponder the results of the work that he got depressed. (I wonder how many medications he would be on if he were alive today?) We can learn something from his experience: find joy, find party, in what we are doing right now. And don't get so hung up on where it's all going. This is a good way to live our lives individually, and especially as we lead together with our teams.

Party People versus Excellence People

Most humans fall into one of two categories: party people or excellence people. You will notice that in this book's list of values, excellence and party are like bookends. Most people are on a continuum between the two, leaning one way or the other. Which one do you naturally lean toward?

If you are not sure, let me help you. Party people like to have fun. They are like my friend Shanna. She lights up every room she enters. She loves people. She loves talking. She loves hugging. She loves conversations and laughter and highlighting everyone's individuality. She often brings cookies or other sweets to band practice. In her opinion, rehearsal is all about the relationships. If we get a song or two practiced, that's cool too, but she wants to make sure we have plenty of time to connect and have fun together.

Excellence people have a different objective: they want to get things done well and in a timely manner. My friend Brandon leans toward excellence. He is always prepared. He loves working on the songs until they are right. He hates the distraction of people talking too much when the team is trying to learn a song. He is always on time, always ready, and always efficient. In his mind, practice is successful when everyone comes to the practice on time prepared and ready to learn the songs proficiently. If we still have time to talk, a few quick conversations are acceptable.

Many times I have walked into band, drama, or other practices at various churches and have spotted the conflict between these two personalities. One of the more profound experiences was with a drama team in Texas. The team leader, Nancy, was a middle-aged woman with a heart for people the size of the state in which she lived. She and two others were on time for practice at 6 p.m. They met in a small room with a large stage, perfect for rehearsal. Their goal was to prepare a sketch they would perform in a church service in the near future. Nancy's concern and love for people were evident from the beginning as she engaged team members with ease, asking them about their families, jobs, homes, cats, dogs, fears, concerns, joys, and dinner plans.

As the rest of the team arrived, I could tell quickly which ones were interested in this kind of conversation. A guy walked in and sat down. Nancy asked about his new job. He took the bait and talked about his boss, the problem with the commute, the lousy hours, and a coworker who was driving him crazy.

Their conversation drew the rest of the team's attention. This guy's admission opened the door for others to ask about how the job was affecting his family and his relationship with Christ.

That, of course, brought more dialogue. As the conversation continued, Nancy decided it would be a good time to pray for this valuable member. She invited anyone to pray. Several did and even laid hands on him.

I glanced at my watch to see that a half-hour had passed. I assumed it was now time to start rehearsing the sketch. But Nancy felt this authentic moment was so strong she needed to press in more. "Anyone else?" she asked.

Sure enough, a woman wanted to talk about how well things were going in her life since she started working out, and another woman wanted to talk about a new friend her daughter met at school. People started laughing and joking and telling funny stories. The energy in the room was picking up, which was good, but by the time the meaningful sharing, chatting, and joking were finally through, it was close to 7 p.m.

Throughout this entire situation, however, a guy named Dave sat in the corner. He did not say a word or crack much of a smile. Instead he kept looking at the sketch in his hands, concentrating and memorizing his lines. Dave had sped from his hectic job as a copyeditor to make it to practice that night, and had a wife and four kids at home waiting for his attention. He also had about an hour's worth of work left to do from his home office. Not only was Dave disinterested in the dialogue unfolding around him, he rolled his eyes a time or two, and occasionally looked around to see if anybody was as irritated as he was about all the time that was being "wasted."

Over the next hour as they finally worked on the sketch, Dave struggled to keep people on track. Several times the group would all start laughing and cutting up about a missed line or a tied tongue, but each time Dave would interrupt the laughing with his next line or a "come on guys" kind of statement.

It was easy to see what was unfolding. The party people, in their minds, were having fun, connecting, and enriching their lives through real relationships. Even the serious, broken tone of the man starting the new job was built out of a party DNA that was clearly in most of the team. But there was one excellence-bent person who was equally concerned with getting the practice done timely and well, also an important value. This illustrates the tension between party people and excellence people. Neither is wrong. They, just like you, have a natural bent, which sometimes causes conflict.

At 8 p.m., as the rehearsal was finishing, Dave left quickly while the rest of the team stood around for another forty-five minutes talking, almost struggling to leave. They were party people who were living the party.

Over time this drama team attracted more and more people who were like its leader, and Dave stopped his involvement. It was a sad situation because Dave was a good, talented person, and the team was not as effective without him. It was also sad because Dave missed out on an opportunity to grow and stretch in the areas of relationship building and fun.

Party people and excellence people don't always see eye to eye. They don't always understand each other and can often cause conflict. So to both groups, I want to articulate clearly: all of the values are equally important. You need people like Dave around to drive you to excellence, and you need people like Nancy around to help people have a great time.

Party people: work a little harder. Come a little more prepared. Be a little more efficient. Don't fill up every second of silence with conversation. Sometimes focus is necessary to get something done well. If Nancy had managed to balance the two types of people, she could have saved some of the relationship building time for later, leaving plenty of energy for focused rehearsal time. Dave would have been stretched to connect and all the partiers would have had more time to give to the practice.

Excellence people: chill out. Or chillax as I more often hear. Laugh a little more. Connect with people a little deeper. Enjoy the moment you are in and realize that not every second has to be planned. Sometimes, by hanging out, we become more effective at what we accomplish together. I know you Daves out there are not necessarily the chillax type. You are looking for ways to make a huge impact in the world and sometimes it seems that living a party gets in the way. Just imagine . . . if Dave would have engaged in the conversation and taken the time to laugh a little with the others, he might have found this out: party people need to laugh and have fun *so they can be excellent*, doing the best with what they have. You see, party people need a party in order to focus on excellence and excellence people need a good healthy working environment to have fun.

By the way, the sketch finally got prepared and performed . . . three months later.

Keeping People Around

One of my best joys is that I have been in ministry with some of the same people for more than fifteen years. The depth of relationship you build over that time is indescribable. One of those people is Mike.

Mike has his fingerprint on the technology of every church that I have led and that Worship Catalyst has served for the past decade and a half. Together we have produced hundreds of services for churches, camps, and other events. One time we had two weeks to put all the sound, video, lighting, and intercom components into our new church building. We worked around the clock to get ready for opening day. We slept at the church, ate at the church, and invited our families to join us so we could see them for a few minutes each day. Sometimes around 3 a.m. when our eyes were so tired we could not see what we were doing, we would force each other to find a chair and get some sleep.

Occasionally Mike and I talk about those two weeks and laugh at what we did. It was crazy; it was exhausting, but we agree that it was one of our most fun times. It was a party! We worked really hard, but we also built a partnership that has extended past multiple states, multiple churches, and many team members.

The idea of this value is that a party culture, balanced with excellence, will lead to people sticking around for a long time. Generally people like having a good time, especially when the rest of their lives are tough. Oftentimes people feel beat up at work or home or in life in general. Most people have heavy responsibilities with bosses or family members that demand a lot of their time and attention. A good team with a party DNA can provide this person with a safe place to feel relief and enjoy life.

On the other hand, sometimes people come to practice from a tough day or week with stresses and challenges. If they get to church where there is nothing but more demands on their time and talent, they might find a better escape at home or somewhere else. It's not that a team at church is supposed to be an escape, but there is no reason it can't be enjoyable. In fact, it *should* feel a lot more like a party than it does a day at work. Second Corinthians 4:10 says that the life of Jesus should be seen in us. We have been bought with a price, rescued from slavery, and assured an eternity with Jesus in heaven. *That* is a party!

Developing a Party DNA

The teams with the highest party values have a few things in common.

First, they build in plenty of time to talk about issues that do not necessarily have to do with church ministry objectives. This happens both spontaneously and intentionally. The team leaders are good at asking questions like, "What has been a great part of your week so far?" or "Anybody heard a good joke lately?"

Second, they are not in a huge hurry to finish. They do not put a ninety-minute deadline on the rehearsal. It is open-ended with a general understanding of approximate time. The rehearsals do not drag on, but they also do not push too hard, as though they are trying to hit a deadline.

Third, they do things outside of church, either just for fun or on mission. As I mentioned earlier, values are not built through events only. However, this value of party has more chance of getting enhanced through events. Have a barbeque at someone's house. Bowl together. Go together on a short-term mission trip, even if it is only for an afternoon. Time as a group is important in enhancing the party DNA.

Fourth, the team has a lot of smiling and laughter. After church one day, my grandmother-in-law asked me why I hated worship leading so much. I told her I didn't hate it; I loved it! And in her soft and gentle way, she said, "Well, you sure didn't look like it!"

It turns out I was singing songs with a frown and maybe even a scowl. Not only was our team lacking a party DNA, I was actually encouraging a sour spirit in the whole church. After that I started making myself smile. It really did change the tone.

As leaders, we are often laser-focused on accomplishing our tasks, which can often lead to a serious, laser-focused face and even culture. Take the time to smile and put your focus on others, not just on the work at hand.

Another habit of teams with a strong party DNA is that they celebrate when things go well. What does a win look like? For us, one of our wins is when we go to God and other people come along with us. When that happens, we celebrate it. When one person brings something especially amazing, we celebrate them and the work of God in them. There is something about pausing to honor a job well done that raises the party value to new heights.

Last, bring cookies or something. It is tough to find a party that does not include food. I have heard experts say that people feel more comfortable and vulnerable when they have something like food or a drink in their hands, so bring something for people to hold and eat. Everybody likes a snack, and the sugar will keep people up and excited—for a few minutes. And then you might want to start practice pretty soon: the crash is coming!

***

What About Us?

1. Between the two values—excellence and party—which one do you naturally lean toward? If you don't know, ask someone to tell you what he or she thinks.

2. Between those two values, which one does your team lean toward the most?

3. What issues might arise between excellence people and party people?

4. How is your team doing on this value of party?

5. What are you planning on doing to elevate this party value on your team?

CHAPTER 10
Making It Stick

In this book you have read many stories of people and teams who realized huge successes in igniting the hearts of their teams. Their successes have come from putting a tight focus on one or more of the values we have discussed. Each of these groups is experiencing renewal and impact in their worship experiences because they have discovered the radical worship solution. It isn't moving lights and fancy smoke machines, professional quality musicians and actors, or even a commitment to the most theologically sound songs or scripts.

The radical worship solution is people like you and me making a life-giving effort to the values of excellence, creativity, unity, humility, authenticity, evangelism, and party. When our teams focus on and truly live out these ideals individually and among one another, we experience God's intention for our churches and for us.

As you process through these values in your life and team, I encourage you to do a few simple things. These impactful actions can be done simultaneously and will not only instill these values in your team, but will cement them into their core DNA.

Review Often

Have you ever seen a professional plate spinner? This performer starts by spinning a plate on a stick. Then he spins another plate on a different stick, and so on until he has ten or more plates all spinning at the same time. Just about the time he gets the last plate going, the first one is slowing down and almost ready to fall. So the spinner runs back to the first plate and spins it quicker just in time to see the one next to it almost fall. He goes from plate to plate, making sure they all have enough energy to keep spinning and not fall and break. It is entertaining and highly stressful.

Sounds like our lives, right? We each have so many different responsibilities—from school to marriage to parenting to career to church. It is often difficult to give each commitment enough energy to keep spinning rather than fall and break. I want to suggest that you see the seven values we discussed as spinning plates.

Now before you break out into a sweat worrying about the value plates all falling, breaking, and ruining your ministry and potentially the lives of many people, let me assure you of something; the plate spinner works alone. You do not. Together, with your team around you, the plates will not fall. With help, you can constantly monitor them, turning one, but also focusing on the others to make sure they aren't left to crash. Also, when the plate spinner succeeds, the crowd cheers, which is cool. But when you succeed, people find real purpose and truly enjoy serving God together with you. That is way better!

Recently I sensed that the value of creativity was waning on our team. We were just going through the motions, planning and performing songs without much thought. The creativity plate was spinning very slowly and showing signs of wobbling. That was not acceptable so I changed two things: (1) we added two new members to our worship planning team and (2) we put someone else—besides me—in charge of band practices. I knew the people we added to the team were creative by nature and always had good ideas. The person I put in charge of the band practices is a good musician and understands music better than I do.

Just those changes were enough to shock us out of our creative slump and start innovating again. While we had been focused on some other values, a quick glance over to creativity revealed that we needed to provide some energy there, getting the plate spinning again.

A good way to keep all the plates spinning is to have consistent conversations with a few people on your team who care deeply about its success and to use the ideas in this book to monitor the growth in the seven values. Just scheduling a time to analyze and talk through it will help your team keep an eye on them all.

Another good way to keep your eye on each of these values is to assign a leader to each one. This "value czar" stays constantly aware of the strength of their particular value and how it is playing out in the team. If it is unity, they could talk often to each person on the team, making sure they connect to other people and feel like they are a real part of the group. They could pray often for each person on the team, asking God to reveal how each one and the team as a whole are doing with unity. They can listen to conversations, making sure no one is experiencing even a hint of disconnectedness or broken relationships. When they sense something unhealthy, this person would have the responsibility to share that with the leaders so unity can be restored and raised even higher.

The idea here is to develop a consistent pattern of analyzing the seven values. In establishing this process, you will not let one of them stop spinning and possibly break, and in so doing limit the effectiveness of the ministry you are trying to build.

So what happens if a plate falls? The fact that you picked up or downloaded this book to read might mean that you have a chronically wobbly or even broken value. First of all, I am sorry. Trust me, I have lived through plenty of broken plates and, honestly, we all will experience them again at some point in our lives. Restoring values is often difficult and takes time and energy. Several years ago I was leading a team whose excellence value went crashing to the ground. It's not like the quality was bad, but everybody knew that excellence was doing the best we could with what we had. We were not. I began to notice a player who showed up to rehearsal without having practiced, another two who gave up on memorizing their music, and a sound guy who had become content with a horrible shrieking sound coming out of the speakers. The plate had been wobbling for a while and I had missed it.

I had some options. I considered getting everybody together and yelling at them. That might have been effective. I could have written a new code of conduct, a Magna Carta of sorts, and forced people to sign the covenant. That might have worked to some degree. But because I had relationships forged over time with each person, I decided to do two things. First, I started talking a lot about excellence, defining it and offering Biblical illustrations of it, similar to the ones in the chapter on excellence. I talked about it at band practice and on Sunday mornings. I also asked my pastor to mention it in a message or two. Second, I had private conversations with these friends to understand what was going on in their lives that would lead to their less-than-excellent performance. We honestly and openly discussed the issues. Ultimately, things picked up and the plate started spinning again.

But plates never spin on their own. It is the focused leader who, at just the right time, gives the plate a good whirl. Alone it is challenging and very difficult to keep an eye on all of them, while putting specialized focus on the one that needs a turn. Plate spinners are winded and sweaty at the end of their routines. But with a team, strategically focused on these values, you will not just keep the plates barely spinning—you will keep them spinning with lots of velocity.

Serve Other Churches

Over the last eight years, all across North America, Worship Catalyst has deployed hundreds of singers, musicians, technologists, actors, and others in order to help new churches get established. These churches and their pioneering pastors often start without worship leaders. And the ones they do have are typically inexperienced and have not had opportunities for much training.

You, as a worship leader, understand how important it is to creatively introduce people to Jesus and to powerfully use music and other art forms. This is where you come in.

What if your team and the teams from other churches decided to serve new churches in your area, filling in as needed, training and even finding and coaching new worship leaders? What if you and your team saw yourselves as worship leaders to the city and not just your church? What if every church in your area became more effective at reaching your community with the gospel and you got to be a part of that? For certain, your team would share a mission and build better relationships, which in turn builds unity. For certain you would have to stretch yourself and learn how to lead in new venues, which builds creativity. You would occasionally participate on very small platforms and serve churches that are not as far along as you, which builds humility. You would be participating in a gospel-centered, rather than local church-centered movement, which builds evangelism. And every person I have sent out over the years has come back and said something like, "That was so much fun and fulfilling. When can I do it again?" They built the value of party!

Sound interesting? Worship Catalyst has hubs of this kind all over North America. People like you in churches like yours are reaching out and making a real difference in their communities. We have the processes, the training, and the deep desire to help you invest in other churches in this way.

Nothing drives the values home more than getting out of the confines of your local church and making an impact on the city and on your church. If you are in any North American city of decent size, you'll find new gospel-centered church families forming all around you. Even if you are in a small community, new churches are probably starting around you as well. Why not help them? Together we can make every church stronger. And the beauty of this is that your team and your church will be healthier and more effective than it has ever been.

Many of the stories in this book came from brand-new churches trying to get better at what they do. All of them were assisted by other people and other church families, many just like yours, who wanted to see them win. Just imagine how exciting it will be for your team to create their own stories of helping other churches in your area. The appendix of this book will give you information on how you can get started.

Ask Daily Questions

In the early 1700s two brothers, John and Charles Wesley, who would later contribute to the formation of the Methodist church, formed a group called the Holy Club. Their idea was that Christians should be notably different from people who were not followers of Christ in the way they live and think. Along the way, they developed a list of twenty-two questions that each club member would ask himself every day. They were introspective questions meant to help guide their thoughts and actions. Many Oxford students, around where the club members lived, criticized this notion of a holy club and the fact that their questions were so internally probing. In fact, they even personally accused the Wesley brothers of being too rules oriented and legalistic.

The critics raised a fair point that Christians can become so legalistic that they focus more on the routine of being a Christian than on the joy and grace a relationship with Jesus offers. But perhaps taking something seriously and doing it to the best of our abilities requires a pattern of some sort. Maybe we are strongest when we consistently analyze how we are doing individually and as a team. If we never look at or analyze the plates that are spinning, we will never notice when they are falling.

With this in mind, our Worship Catalyst team set out on a mission to create a list of questions that would help worship leaders like you and me determine how we are doing at internalizing and living out the seven values. We took some of the Wesleys' Holy Club questions and then added our own and arranged them around those values.

In the chapter about humility, I recounted a story in which my pride got the best of me when a fellow team member talked a lot about discipleship. I recognized that pride quickly because I was in the pattern of daily asking myself four questions about humility.

If you will make these questions a part of your daily and weekly life, you will start to notice more clearly and quickly when you are living outside of the seven values.

Excellence

Ask yourself daily:

> * Did I give God my best today (in my craft, my time, my appearance, and in every other area)?
> * Did I help others get better at what they do?

Ask yourself weekly:

> * Am I a slave to dress, friends, work, or habits?
> * Am I defeated in any area of my life?

Creativity

Ask yourself daily:

* Did I notice the creativity of God?

* Did I do anything creative (in any area)?

Ask yourself weekly:

* Am I allowing fear of what others would say limit
my creativity?

Unity

Ask yourself daily:

* Was I jealous, critical, irritable, or touchy?

* Did I pass on to another anything that was told to
me in confidence?

Ask yourself weekly:

* Is there anyone whom I fear, dislike, disown,
criticize, resent, or disregard? If so, what am I
doing about it?

Authenticity

Ask yourself daily:

* Did I consciously or unconsciously create the impression
that I am better than I really am? In other words, am I a
hypocrite?

* Was I honest in all my acts and words, or did I exaggerate?

* Did I allow time for God's Word to speak to me?

* Did I disobey God in anything?

Ask yourself weekly:

   * Am I enjoying prayer?

Humility

Ask yourself daily:

   * Did I critique very closely the work of other people in my field, matching myself against them?

   * Did I try to stand out in a crowd (through the way I talk or play or sing or act or dress) because I wanted everybody to know how good I am at something? Did I use big words and try to sound smart?

Ask yourself weekly:

   * Have I acted self-conscious, self-pitying, or self-justifying?

   * When someone else is receiving accolades, am I inwardly frustrated, wishing I would get some praise?

   * When someone else gets credit for something I secretly did, do I want to let everyone know that I am the one who did it?

Evangelism

Ask yourself daily:

   * Am I actively building relationships with and praying for people who are far from God?

Ask yourself weekly:

   * When did I last speak to someone else about my faith?

Party

Ask yourself daily:

* Did I help others enjoy life?

Ask yourself weekly:

* Am I enjoying life?

You Made It!

As I mentioned earlier, I have started and not finished a whole bookshelf of great books. But you finished. Congratulations! You will be better for it.

We began this journey with a band practice that had gone critically wrong. The team had lost sight of every value. Hopefully, over the course of this book, and in the appendix to follow, you and your team have had a chance to discuss how you are doing in the areas of excellence, creativity, unity, humility, authenticity, evangelism, and party. If you will commit to these values and slowly raise them in your team, I am convinced that together you will be more effective at your goal: going to God and taking others with you. Your church will have found the radical worship solution. You will have begun to ignite the heart of your team and church.

***

What About Us?

1. What is the most impactful thing you learned while reading this book?

2. Which of the seven values does your team need to spend the most time on? Which plate is spinning the most slowly?

3. As you read through the daily and weekly questions, which value jumped out to you as the one(s) you personally need to put some energy into?

4. How might your team be equipped to serve new churches in your area? Does this sound like a mission your team could rally around?

APPENDIX
Catalyzing Worship in Your City

As I mentioned in chapter 10, the best way to make the radical worship solution values stick is to put them into action by serving new churches. What kind of team should take on a challenge like this?

First, it is a team that is willing and eager to partner with other churches to reach its community. Every Worship Catalyst expression across North America is a collaboration of multiple churches with a team of people who can pitch in at various levels of involvement—more on that in a moment. So even if your church is not huge with dozens of talented people at every position, you can still participate, and even lead the charge.

Second, it is a team that cares about other churches and believes that one church is not enough to reach their community.

Third, it is a team that is willing to walk with a new church through a process of worship-team and worship-leader development.

Fourth, it is a team that wants to become part of a nationwide movement of believers committed to impacting their city, not just their church.

If this sounds like an intriguing idea for your team, then let me explain how it works. While I don't have the space here to give you the full-scale development program (that would take another book!), I do want to help you understand the basic principles of what serving other churches looks like. As is the case for much of this book, I will explain it in a real-life example of one of the churches our Worship Catalyst team has helped.

A new church was emerging in a suburban city in Arizona. The leaders, Steve and Jay, were new to the area and didn't know where to turn to find singers, musicians, and technologists for their worship services. Worship Catalyst has relationships with church-planting organizations and groups in the Tucson area as we do in all of our hub cities. Through those relationships, I heard that Steve and Jay were starting a new church so I quickly called them to set up a meeting. After a conversation over Sonoran Mexican food, a Tucson-area staple, it became apparent that I would need to call on several members of my Worship Catalyst Tucson team to serve. This team was made up of about twenty singers, musicians, and technologists from multiple churches who were willing to pitch in and help a new church get started. Most of them were involved in their own local churches, but rotated out some weeks, which made them available to serve in other places.

Steve and Jay needed help in multiple areas. Though we could have potentially done five or six things at once (such as train sound people, hold a worship planning workshop, etc), we narrowed our short-term focus to three main areas of activity:

1. Find a sound system for them to use.

2. Provide people to fill in as singers/guitar players for their services.

3. Identify other people in their community and church who could play or sing so they could have their own band.

I contacted our team's tech leader, Mike, and he quickly found a sound system that would work perfectly for this new church. The speakers and sound board were in good working order but had been in a closet at another church in town, unused for more than a year.

I then talked to several people from the team, made sure they were able to play or sing once per month in this new church, and then put them on a rotation. We promised the church pastors that we would not let them go without music for even one week.

Having secured a sound system and a rotation of worship leaders, it was time to start building a team for that church. First, I looked within. Steve and Jay had built their core team to about twenty-five adults, plus their children. I asked around and found out that one teenage son and one of the adults had some background in playing drums and running sound. I met with them to determine if they could get to the needed ability level to be on the team. Since the team had virtually no one on it, the bar was not set super high.

I also started looking around the community. I put up a few notices on Craigslist and searched through some other music websites and quickly got connected to two other Christian musicians—a guitar player and a bassist—who lived close by. I got together with these two musicians, plus the drummer from the core team, and we played some music, built a relationship, and started weekly practices. Sometimes I led the practice and sometimes someone else from my team led it. Before long, we had a list of songs that we could play, and we debuted on a Sunday several weeks later.

A few months into this process, a young man with some experience as a singer and guitar player moved from Steve and Jay's hometown to Arizona to go to college. This presented a great opportunity for the church and for us to invest in a young man who had some potential to lead the church in worship. We started walking this young man through the worship-leader development process I mentioned in chapter 2 called "Worship Leader Essentials." Within months he was blending into the team well and was able to take over. My team and I bowed out, said goodbye, and pointed our efforts elsewhere. In all, we spent around a year with this church and deployed more than a dozen people to serve them as they got started.

Although every church has a different set of specific worship needs as they begin, Steve and Jay's is a pretty common story. We assessed the need, made a plan, and then worked the plan with the ultimate goal of helping the church have a self-sustaining and growing team.

Now What?

If this sounds intriguing for your team, it is time for a conversation. Reach out to me at Austin@WorshipCatalyst.com and we can talk further about what it would take for you and your team to make a city impact by serving new churches. We have processes and steps that you would need to join many others in leading the charge to build a team to serve churches like Steve's and Jay's. We call this a Worship Catalyst Hub.

It was interesting to watch my team deploy to this suburban Tucson church. Some of the new ones went a bit sheepishly, maybe even scared, but as they came back, week by week, you could see their confidence and faith in God grow. The greatest benefit is that without even having to talk too much about it, the values we have discussed in this book took root deeply into their lives. If you will take the next step toward joining this cause, you will not only make a real gospel impact on your region, you will also reenergize and ignite the heart of your team. I look forward to hearing from you!

Notes

Chapter 3: Excellence

[1] Jeff Syzmanski, as told to Carey Goldberg, "When Perfectionism Becomes a Problem," Boston Globe, March 2, 2009, http://www.boston.com/lifestyle/articles/2009/03/02/when_perfectionism_becomes_a_problem/?page=full.

Chapter 4: Creativity

[1] Anne Marie Helmenstine, "How Many Atoms Are in the Human Body," http://chemistry.about.com/od/biochemistry/a/How-Many-Atoms-Are-In-The-Human-Body.htm.

[2] Hartmut Frommert and Christine Kronberg, "The Milky Way Galaxy," August 25, 2005, http://messier.seds.org/more/mw.html.

[3] Julie Eilperin, "8.7 Million Species Exist on Earth, Study Estimates," Washington Post, August 23, 2011, http://www.washingtonpost.com/national/health-science/87-million-species-exist-on-earth-study-estimates/2011/08/22/gIQAE7aZZJ_story.html.

[4] "New Plant and Fungus Species Discovered," Science Daily, June 5, 2012, http://www.sciencedaily.com/releases/2012/06/120605172021.htm.

[5] Mario Vaden, "Coast Redwoods Year of Discovery," http://www.mdvaden.com/redwood_year_discovery.shtml.

[6] "Heart Facts," Cleveland Clinic, http://my.clevelandclinic.org/services/heart/heart-blood-vessels/heart-facts.

[7] Worldometers, http://www.worldometers.info/world-population/.

[8] Jim Collins, Good to Great (New York, NY: HarperBusiness, 2001).

[9] http://www.forbes.com/sites/afontevecchia/2013/03/26/hedge-fund-billionaire-steve-cohens-155m-picasso-isnt-his-first-multi-million-piece-of-art/.

Chapter 5: Unity

[1] Kenneth Copeland, "What in the World Is 'The Anointing'?," KCM.org, http://www.kcm.org/read/questions/what-the-world-%E2%80%9Cthe-anointing%E2%80%9D.

[2] The definitions for glory are from the following Bible dictionaries, in order of appearance: Holman Concise Bible Dictionary, Holman Bible Dictionary, The Ultimate Bible Dictionary, Easy English Bible Dictionary.

[3] All Scripture verses in this paragraph are taken from the New International Version (NIV).

Chapter 8: Evangelism

[1] "The Top 10 Causes of Death," World Health Organization, http://www.who.int/mediacentre/factsheets/fs310/en/index2.html.

Acknowledgments

I have read the first half of many books and typically shoot right past the acknowledgments page, unless I know the person. Then I think that just maybe I said something amazing or profound in their life, and they remembered it just as they were writing their thanks. But I will never pass that section again. I finally understand what it means. This book, as I am sure is the case of most books, is the outcome of decades of investments that people have made in me. I must be the most fortunate, most invested-in guy in the world. So if I may, I want to thank, in no particular order . . . it doesn't mean anything if one person is first or third or last or whatever . . . everyone is important . . . I am even driving home that point by putting Jesus somewhere in the middle . . .

Cami, my wife. Okay, she's first for a reason. For twenty years she has been my bride, and she has been my best friend for way longer than that. She refines me, challenges me, keeps me motivated, and makes me a more disciplined person. As for this book, it functionally would not have happened without her reads, re-reads, edits, and her soothing way of saying that a particular part was either genius or stupid. I love you, Cami. Especially when you are honest enough to call something stupid.

Finley Ryan, my wife's and my only offspring. She is energetic, talented, full of life, and keeps me feeling either really young or really old. Mostly she loves her mom and me and Jesus all the time and gives us more joy than we can imagine. Life is better because of her. I love you, Pantalones.

Ben Barfield, my pastor, ministry partner, Worship Catalyst board member, and friend. We have been part of planting two churches together and pushing the boundaries of what is acceptable or permissible in church. I think we might have even passed up that boundary a time or two. The Radical Worship Solution is pushed along more efficiently when it includes a pastor who embodies every aspect of it. Thanks, Ben.

Tommy and Carolyn Ryan, my mom and dad. I could literally fill a whole book about what these two folks have done in me. I am who I am because of them. Their belief in me, support no matter what, encouragement, and guidance have given me confidence my whole life. From childhood to today, I can see their fingerprints all over everything I have touched. Plus, they have been married for well over fifty years—a great roadmap to follow! I love you guys.

The amazing supporters of Worship Catalyst. When Cami and I started this ministry, we stepped into a new world of support raising and faith we had never experienced. The faithful, sacrificial, financial investments and prayers of many people and churches have made possible the transformation of many, many new churches. Cami and I will never take you for granted.

Jesus, the only one who has ever died in my place. I am not sure how you write an acknowledgment for the Savior of the world without sounding trite or perfunctory. But honestly, from the bottom of my heart, I am first and foremost your servant and ready to do whatever you want me to do next. It's worked out 100 percent of the time.

Ginger Kolbaba, our editor and now friend. She has crazy, mad, genious skills when it comes to reading something that looks sort of like a sentence or paragraph and making it sound like somebody smart wrote it. Thanks for joining our team, Ginger. This couldn't have happened without you.

Wes Spiegel and the rest of the Worship Catalyst board. Cami and I lead under the accountability and mentorship of this great group of people. Most of them have been with us from day one and we are in debt to them in many ways. Wes, our chairman, thanks for the Monday mornings at Harris County BBQ. Margaret Menger, Anthony Diaz, Chase Sligh, Ben, Kyle Bell, and former board members Rick Black and Troy Gaddie, thanks for your friendship and leadership in my life.

Larry Womack and the rest of the people at Copperfield Church, as well as the people of Common Ground Arizona. Somehow God has always put me around success. Copperfield and Common Ground are both stories of faith. Copperfield taught me how to trust Jesus to provide for everything. Common Ground taught me to believe in miracles. Thank you all for trusting in what we do and investing deeply in me. *left blank intentionally*

Made in the USA
Middletown, DE
20 October 2016